Exploring the Connection Between

MORMONS

AND

MASONS

OTHER BOOKS AND AUDIO BOOKS
BY MATTHEW B. BROWN:

A PILLAR OF LIGHT

RECEIVING GIFTS OF THE SPIRIT

JOSEPH SMITH: THE MAN, THE MISSION, THE MESSAGE

SYMBOLS IN STONE: SYMBOLISM ON THE EARLY TEMPLES OF THE RESTORATION

THE GATE OF HEAVEN: INSIGHTS ON THE DOCTRINES AND SYMBOLS OF THE TEMPLE

THE PLAN OF SALVATION: DOCTRINAL NOTES AND COMMENTARY

ALL THINGS RESTORED: EVIDENCES AND WITNESSES OF THE RESTORATION

PLATES OF GOLD: THE BOOK OF MORMON COMES FORTH

PROPHECIES: SIGNS OF THE TIMES, SECOND COMING, MILLENNIUM

Exploring the Connection Between

MORMONS

AND

MASONS

MATTHEW B. BROWN

Covenant Communications, Inc.

Jacket design by Jessica A. Warner.
Cover image lineart courtesy of Grand Lodge of British Colombia and Yukon. For information please
visit www.freemasonry.bcy.ca/graphics.html.

Cover design copyrighted 2009 by Covenant Communications, Inc.

Published by Covenant Communications, Inc.
American Fork, Utah

Printed in Canada
First Printing: September 2009

16 15 14 13 12 11 10 09   10 9 8 7 6 5 4 3

ISBN-13: 978-1-59811-893-3
ISBN-10: 1-59811-893-5

CONTENTS

INTRODUCTION

The subject of Joseph Smith and Freemasonry is one that rarely reaps a dull verbal or emotional response in a crowd. Looks of curiosity, revulsion, frustration, and outright excitement can be seen on the faces of conversationalists as they wend their way through the rugged terrain of this subject's history, theology, traditional understandings, and myths. There are typically more questions raised than answers given on this complex topic, but there never seems to be a shortage of opinion about it.

No matter what form the questions take, and no matter what side of the fence they are coming from, they are deserving of contemplation, some of them calling for in-depth investigation. Why did Joseph Smith become a Freemason? Who introduced Freemasonry into Nauvoo, Illinois, in the early 1840s? Do the Masons really descend from the workmen who built King Solomon's Temple? What is the relationship between the Masonic lodge and the Mormon temple?

This book has been written as a guide of sorts to assist the student of the past in separating out some of the facts from the fiction. While it is not possible to cover every topic associated with Joseph Smith and Freemasonry in this volume, the contents will deal with the core issues. Hopefully by the end of this book, readers will not only feel that they have advanced in their understanding but also come to the realization that the conversation on this issue has taken a few significant steps forward.

This volume consists of seven chapters and two appendices. It begins by providing definitions regarding the two ritual systems under discussion and supplying sufficient details about them so that meaningful comparisons can then be made between the two.

The second chapter focuses on the verifiable history of the Freemasons as opposed to their mythology. It is crucial to have an accurate understanding of this organization's past if one desires to discern its true nature. This chapter is useful in helping the researcher to see something of how this organization gradually morphed into its present state.

Chapter three is one of the most important parts of this book. The line of historical descent for the Masonic craft is fairly well established, but the pedigree of what the Freemasons do is problematic. The material in this part of the book should clarify the question to a marked degree and in turn answer the critical question of where speculative Freemasonry ultimately comes from. This knowledge, in turn, will help to clarify and explain Joseph Smith's relationship to Freemasonry.

The fourth chapter centers on Nauvoo, Illinois, and the founding of the Nauvoo Lodge in March 1842. It also reveals the level of the Prophet Joseph Smith's activity in the lodge between the time he became a Freemason and the introduction of the full LDS temple endowment in May 1842. The question of whether Joseph Smith was actually made a Mason "at sight" is addressed on these pages.

Chapter five is called "Return to Mount Zion." This was the name of the mountain in ancient Jerusalem upon which the temple of the Lord was constructed. The material in this portion of the book consists of a historical timeline detailing what Joseph Smith knew about temples and temple worship before he became a Freemason. The pieces of data that have been included in this timeline are detailed but should not be considered exhaustive (there is much more information that pertains to this area of historical inquiry). This chapter is all about seeing the bigger picture so that more accurate assessments of the past can be made.

In the sixth chapter, the reader will be taken into the upper room of Joseph Smith's redbrick store, which was used as a

temporary Masonic lodge room as well as a provisional temple—
along with many other purposes. The text will explain the ecclesiastical and Masonic standings of all the brethren who received
the Nauvoo endowment on 4 May 1842 and what their reac-
tions were after their experience.

Did the First Presidency of the Church write in 1911 that
the temple ceremony contained "Masonic characters"? Were
there no contemplated changes between the Kirtland and
Nauvoo Temple ordinances until after Joseph Smith became a
Freemason? Did Joseph Smith intend to restore Freemasonry to
its pure form? Did Brigham Young really call the endowment
"Celestial Masonry"? Were Masonic decorative and functional
patterns incorporated into the Kirtland and Nauvoo Temples?
Is there a Masonic prayer written on the front of the original
Relief Society minute book? Did Joseph Smith have knowledge
of Masonic secrets long before he joined the Freemasons? The
seventh chapter of the present volume is perhaps one of the
more provocative because it addresses these and other interesting issues and also deals heavy blows to several long-standing
myths (among Saints and critics alike). It is also geared toward
providing enlightenment on several important points.

Two appendices offer further information at the end of this
book. The first appendix is designed to show that even though
some people are sure that the symbols on the exterior of the Salt
Lake Temple must be Masonic, the emblems were being utilized
by the Saints long before the Masons dedicated the Nauvoo
Lodge. The second appendix is a brief collection of quotes and
summations from nineteenth-century Latter-day Saints that lay
out their view regarding the relationship between the ritual practices of Freemasonry and the blessings of the house of the Lord.

It is my sincere hope that those people who explore what is
written in this manuscript will do so in the spirit of learning "by
study and also by faith" (D&C 88:118). Hidden treasures of
knowledge await the persevering seeker.

AUTHOR'S NOTE: *Unless otherwise specified, all quotations in this book that originate in historical sources have been standardized to conform to modern standards of spelling, punctuation, capitalization, and grammar.*

CHAPTER 1

The Lord's House
and the Mason's Lodge

Mormons have been engaged in temple building since the early 1830s, while lodges for stonemasons have been erected for members of that profession at least as far back as the Middle Ages. The perceived connection between these two institutions has been a matter of declaration, speculation, and debate since the early 1840s. Anyone who becomes immersed in this topic quickly learns that it is no simple matter to understand.

Perhaps the best thing to do in approaching this subject is to start by asking simple questions about Mormon temples and Masonic lodges and providing answers from authoritative and reputable sources. Since Latter-day Saints hold their temples and associated ordinances to be of an especially sacred nature, this book will be careful to only mention such matters that have been openly discussed in official Church publications and in the *Encyclopedia of Mormonism*. Even then, the details will be kept to a minimum. When it comes to Masonic lodges and the rites performed therein, the rules of common courtesy will be applied. The Masons desire to keep some of their proceedings private, and this book is not meant to be an exposé of what they do. Again, material that is used in describing the Freemasons and their ways will only be gleaned from sources that are respected.

THE HOUSE OF THE LORD

An insightful and efficient way to learn about the nature of Latter-day Saint temples is to answer a series of simple inquiries. Ten of the most common questions posed about the house of the Lord are as follows.

What is the chief characteristic of the temple? All Latter-day Saint temples are of a decidedly religious character. The land upon which they are built is dedicated by prayer. Religious symbols and paintings are used to adorn them. A plaque on the exterior of each temple reads, HOLINESS TO THE LORD. They are considered to be holy ground. They are consecrated by prayer, after which celebrants shout joyful hosannas to God and the Lamb. The ordinances performed there are all religious by nature.

Why do Mormons build temples? As part of the Restoration of the gospel of Jesus Christ in the dispensation of the fullness of times, the Prophet Joseph Smith received direct commandments to construct houses of the Lord. A command was issued separately for the temples in Independence, Missouri (see D&C 57:1–3); Kirtland, Ohio (see D&C 95:8); Far West, Missouri (see D&C 115:8); and Nauvoo, Illinois (see D&C 124:31). Mormons build temples, therefore, because of divine decree. The reason for such a heavenly directive was mentioned by Elder Charles C. Rich, who stated that temples are built by the Saints because God "ordained from before the foundation of our world . . . that His people can only receive from Him certain blessings in certain places."[1]

Whom are they dedicated to? This question was answered by President Howard W. Hunter, who taught that "the temples we dedicate are dedicated to our Heavenly Father. These temples are His houses, built in His name for His glory and for His purposes."[2] Elder David B. Haight explained that Deity's ownership of a temple is not figurative but that each temple "is literally a house of the Lord—a place where He and His Spirit may dwell, where He may come or send others."[3]

Who is allowed to enter within their walls? Before LDS temples are formally dedicated, they are open to public tours, and persons of all faiths are welcome. After the dedication, however, only those people who have received prerequisite ordinances (if they have reached the age or stage of accountability) and who have been interviewed to ascertain conformance with gospel standards may enter and participate in the ritual and administrative aspects of the sanctuary.[4] Patrons include both men and women and span in age from infants to the elderly. Some women officiators are given "priesthood responsibility" to administer certain "priesthood ordinances" in "priesthood power," though they are not ordained to the priesthood or to any of its offices.[5]

What is the setting of the temple? Mormon temples are not considered to be elaborate mock-ups or stage props but rather authentic sanctuaries of the Most High God. The ordinances practiced therein are believed to be a restoration of things that were done in the time of the patriarchs Adam, Noah, and Abraham,[6] and also in the Tabernacle fashioned by the prophet Moses and the temple built by King Solomon (see D&C 124:37–38). The Prophet Joseph Smith taught that such things were also practiced during the dispensation of the Messiah.[7] Like the Israelite temples of the Bible, the Spirit of God is palpably present inside of the Mormon structures, and they are houses of divine revelation like in days of old.

What takes place inside temples? A generalized list of ceremonial activities in the temple is as follows: baptism, confirmation, priesthood ordination (for men), washings and anointings, reception of sacred clothing, endowments (which includes instruction, covenants, and prayer), and sealings (for marriage and families).[8]

What are temple activities centered upon? The *Encyclopedia of Mormonism* states succinctly that "all temple ordinances point to Christ."[9] By participating in the temple ordinances, a patron imitates the actions of Jesus Christ and shares in His powers and blessings. The Lord was baptized and received the gift—or endowment—of the Holy Spirit (see Matt. 3:16). He also attained priestly status (see Heb. 4:14). The washings and anointings "signify the cleansing and sanctifying power of Jesus Christ applied to the attributes of the person."[10] The clothing "symbolizes Christ-like attributes in one's mission in life."[11] The temple endowment proper "constitutes a major part of the overwhelming gift extended to humanity through the Atonement of Christ."[12] Couples in the temple are "married through the sealing power of Jesus Christ,[13] and family sealings lead ultimately to attachment to "the family of Adam, which becomes the family of Jesus Christ."[14] Persons who perform temple service by proxy are given the opportunity to share in the Master's great vicarious work of salvation by acting in the role of "saviors" on Mount Zion.[15]

What type of authority sanctions the proceedings there? The president of the LDS Church possesses the power bestowed anciently by Jesus Christ to bind something on earth and have that thing bound in heaven or, in other words, be valid and binding after death.[16] The Prophet Joseph Smith connected this sealing power with the fullness of the Melchizedek Priesthood.[17]

What is the scope of the work that is carried out in those places? The scope of time for things that take place in the temple includes the past, present, and future. Hence, President James E. Faust once said, "The solemn mysteries of where we came from, why we are here, and where we are going are answered more fully in the temples."[18] The Lord's house is also connected with two different spatial dimensions. Those who live on the earth receive their personal blessings, and then they offer the same, by proxy, to those persons who have passed into the world of spirits. In Mormon theology, "all the ordinances that are essential for the salvation of the living are likewise essential for the dead."[19]

What purposes do the temples ultimately serve? According to Elder Bruce R. McConkie, "all temple ordinances, except baptism for the dead, pertain to exaltation in the celestial kingdom and not merely to admission to that world."[20] Without the temple ordinances, said the Prophet Joseph Smith, the Saints "cannot obtain celestial thrones."[21] And in the words of President Ezra Taft Benson, "The temple ceremony was given by a wise Heavenly Father to help us become more Christ-like."[22]

THE LODGE OF THE MASONS

A basic understanding of the nature of Freemasonry can now be obtained by asking the same set of ten questions applied to Mormon temples. A comparison of the two institutions can then be made in order to determine, on a general level, what similarities and differences exist between them. The information below is based only on the three basic degrees of Craft Masonry since those were the only ones that were conferred upon Joseph Smith Jr.

What is the chief characteristic of a Masonic lodge? The United Grand Lodge of England defines Freemasonry as a "secular" fraternal organization and emphasizes that it is not a religion or a substitute for religion and does not allow discussions about religion to take place during its meetings.[23] The lodge itself and the first three Masonic initiation ceremonies, however, are filled with biblical and Christian symbolism and references.

Why do Masons build lodges? Freemasons construct lodges so that they can have a private place to meet and conduct a variety of business transactions regarding administration, training, initiation, and discipline. The lodges of medieval and later operative masons were sheds or lean-tos where architectural tools were stored, stones were shaped, and recreational activities took place. Very simple initiation rites were performed inside of these early lodges.[24]

Who are lodges dedicated to? Masonic lodges are typically dedicated to "the Saints John," which means Saint John the Baptist and Saint John the Evangelist. "In the sixteenth century St. John the Baptist seems to have been considered as the peculiar patron of Freemasonry; but subsequently this honor was divided between the two Saints John." Near the beginning of the twentieth century in the United States of America lodges were "universally erected or consecrated to God, and dedicated to the Holy Saints John."[25]

Who is allowed to enter within lodge walls? Normally, only men are initiated into Masonic lodges. During times of ceremonial work, only a set number of officiators, spectators/participants who have received the degree of initiation being performed, and the candidate are allowed to be present in the lodge room. All others are kept at bay by a door guard who is called a Tiler.

The prerequisites for admittance to the Masonic fraternity are being "of good repute" and having "a belief in a Supreme Being" that is associated with any type of spiritual faith.[26] In the time of Joseph Smith, membership was determined first by approval from a three-man committee of investigations and then by anonymous balloting by the recognized members of the lodge where the application was made.

Some Masonic buildings are occasionally utilized for events that are not of a Masonic character, and the general public is free to enter during those times.[27]

What is the setting of the lodge? The Masonic initiate is told that his induction into the three degrees of Craft Masonry is taking place figuratively in the courtyard, Holy Place, and Holy of Holies of the biblical temple built by King Solomon. It is made clear during the initiation that the mimicked Old Testament temple of the lodge is not in a finished state but is in the process of being constructed. When the initiate makes a participatory connection to the temple near the end of the three degrees experience, he disassociates himself from present time and takes part in a biblically-based but legendary tale. "The Masonic idea of the Temple," says one historian of the Craft, is "entirely symbolic. The Temple is to the speculative Mason only a symbol, not an historical building."[28]

What takes place inside of Masonic lodges? The United Grand Lodge of England states that precepts are taught to initiates of Freemasonry "by a series of ritual dramas, which follow ancient forms, and use stonemasons' customs and tools as allegorical guides."[29] This same source reports that Masonic initiates are taught about gaining "self-knowledge," and they also learn a number of moral lessons while they are being inducted.[30]

There are three fundamental levels of Masonic initiation that correspond to three levels of the stonemason's trade: Entered Apprentice, Fellow Craft, and Master Mason. The candidate is given a piece of clothing that is modified as he progresses through these rites. He is taught about different architectural symbols, and in the third degree he learns about a biblical character from the Solomonic time period.[31]

What are Masonic activities centered on? Freemasons strive to inculcate the principles of brotherly love, relief or charity, and truth in their members. The goal in following these ideals is declared to be "achieving higher standards in life."[32]

It has been pointed out by one Masonic writer that these "are all tenets shared with other communities, especially religious ones."[33]

What type of authority sanctions the proceedings in a lodge? There is no central group that governs all of Freemasonry. However, the authority for a local lodge to function is granted by the Grand Lodge of a particular geographic region or jurisdiction. Some countries (such as England, Ireland, and Scotland) have a Grand Lodge over the entire nation, while in the United States there is a Grand Lodge presiding over each state.[34]

What is the scope of the work that is carried out in a lodge? The three basic Masonic rites experienced by the candidate present the perspective of ancient biblical characters and the medieval stoneworker's guild, and also the perspective of the present day. The officiators in the lodge take on roles that pertain to both past and present time frames. The Masonic rites point toward a future existence that lies beyond mortality.[35]

What purposes do the lodges ultimately serve? A widely promoted catchphrase of Freemasonry says that the organization exists in order to "make good men better." The overall goal of the Masonic ceremonies (which is emphasized through symbolic costume and action) is to bring a person from a state of figurative darkness to one of light.[36] There is an expectation in many (but not all) forms of Freemasonry that the application of Masonic initiation principles to one's life will result in being allowed, after death, to go to the Grand Lodge Above and be in the presence of the Grand Architect of the Universe.

COMPARISONS

Now that the same set of ten questions has been asked about Mormon temples and Masonic lodges it is possible to make general comparisons between these two institutions and thereby ascertain some of their similarities and differences.[37]

The fundamental natures of the two institutions (as presently constituted) are completely opposite each other. The temple is a place of religious practice while the lodge declares itself to be a secular organization. It should be noted, however, that medieval operative Masonry was closely associated with European Catholicism, but its Christian character was eroded after the formation of the speculative Grand Lodge of England in the year 1717.

The reason for the existence of the two institutions is also noticeably different. The lodges of the speculative Masons exist because of the desire for men to join in the fraternal bonds of brotherhood and to make a positive difference in society. The Mormon temples, on the other hand, have come into being because God has ordered their construction so that He might facilitate certain aspects of His eternal plan for mankind.

The dedication of the two types of buildings is of interest because they seem, in a partial sense at least, to overlap. All Mormon temples are dedicated to God the Father, and so are some of the Masonic lodges. However, that is where the similarity ends. The Masons of any particular lodge may pay homage to any number of deities of many different types, whereas the Mormon temples are dedicated solely to the Father of Jesus of Nazareth. The Masonic practice of dedicating lodges to John the Baptist and John the Evangelist is a vestige of Masonry's once-close connection to the Roman Catholic Church. The two Johns function as patron Saints of Freemasonry.

Admittance to lodges and temples is markedly different. Both organizations require that a candidate pass through the scrutiny of one's personal character. The Masons, however, interview the candidate and his friends, neighbors, and colleagues in order to ascertain whether they should be admitted, while the Mormons are interviewed themselves only—twice (and repeatedly on a two-year basis). The Mormons must adhere to a specific health code to gain admission while the Masons do not. The Masons pay a fee to enter while the Mormons pay a tithe on all of their income annually. Women are not allowed to participate in traditional Masonic initiations but the participation of women in the temple is an absolute necessity.

It is apparent that the temples of The Church of Jesus Christ of Latter-day Saints are genuine houses of the Lord, while the Masonic lodges do not attempt to take upon themselves such a lofty and holy status. The "temple" of the Freemasons is just an allegorical instructional device, whereas the Mormon temple is a replica of the hallowed sanctuaries of biblical times.

Mormons and the Masons practice ordinances and rituals, respectively, inside their buildings. Each set of rites includes the elements of drama and instruction and vows and symbolism. Indeed, both groups use an altar and have officiators to guide them through the ceremonies. Yet, the personal connection with the rites is divergent for the two sets of people. The Freemasonic initiate is to briefly connect himself with the Solomonic era of the Bible, while Latter-day Saints reach back to the very beginning of that sacred text to forge their connection.

The idea of "centering" can be found in both the Mormon and Masonic systems. The Mormons have a vertically oriented center. The LDS temple rituals are meant to point one toward, and connect one with, the Savior of mankind. The Masons, on the other hand, have a horizontally oriented center in that they are focused primarily on mankind and their personal advancement within the Masonic organization. It needs to be pointed out once again that some Masonic lodges teach their candidates that the practice of speculative Masonry will play a role in how they will experience the afterlife. But in old Masonic texts this ideology is clearly based on information from the New Testament and can thus be seen as another vestige of the original Christian nature of Freemasonry.

Authority is a very important theme in both the Mormon and Masonic institutions. But again, the disparity lies in the fact that the LDS temple operates under authorized priesthood representatives who are acting in the name of the Lord Jesus Christ, while the Freemasons administrate from a strictly secular point of view and only with a power that originated on the earth.

Another difference between lodge and temple is the scope of the work carried out in each. When a Freemason is initiated, he is presented with information that pertains to the present and a small portion of the biblical past. He only receives a brief, and very general, hint about the postmortal future. The Latter-day Saint experience is quite different. They are immersed in primordial time. They see things not only from the vantage point of the far distant (even premortal) past and the present, but are also taught very specific things that pertain to the post-resurrection future. Furthermore, the ordinances of the temple presently encompass the realm of the dead as well as that of the living. There is no such thing as proxy work for the dead among the Freemasons.

Finally, there is the issue of overall purpose. The Mason's lodge is principally designed to make good men better and thereby enhance their mortal lives. Many Freemasons believe that their fraternal membership will prepare them for what is to come after they die (despite the stance that Freemasonry is not a religion). The Mormon temple is designed to take both men and women many steps further than the concept of general salvation by giving them the opportunity to achieve exaltation together in eternity. The supreme aim of the temple is to change mortals who are now in a fallen state into truly Christlike beings.

Ultimately, it can be said that the temple and the lodge have the same basic aim of improving individuals during mortality, but only one of these institutions has the sanction of God and the necessary sacred space, power, and ordinances that will enable them to reach their full eternal potential.

NOTES

1. Conference Report, April 1880, 88.

2. *New Era,* April 1995, 9.

3. *Ensign,* November 1990, 59.

4. Daniel H. Ludlow, ed., *Encyclopedia of Mormonism* (New York: Macmillan, 1992), 4:1446; hereafter cited as *EM*.

5. Ibid., 3:1137.

6. On 5 October 1840 Joseph Smith said that God revealed to Adam a "plan of ordinances for the salvation of his posterity" and subsequently the Lord gave Noah the "the keys, the covenants, the power, and the glory with which he blessed Adam at the beginning" (Andrew F. Ehat and Lyndon W. Cook, eds., *The Words of Joseph Smith: The Contemporary Accounts of the Nauvoo Discourses of the Prophet Joseph*, rev. ed. [Orem, UT: Grandin Book, 1991], 39, 42; hereafter cited as *WJS*). On 27 August 1843 the Prophet Joseph Smith taught that "Abraham . . . received . . . the last law or a fullness of the law or priesthood which constituted him a king and priest after the order of Melchizedek" (ibid., 246).

7. The Prophet said that Jesus Christ received "the fullness of [the] priesthood or the law of God" on the Mount of Transfiguration (ibid.). On 11 June 1843 the Prophet specified that Jesus Christ obtained "the fullness of God" by "keeping all the ordinances of the house of the Lord." He further stated on this occasion that the Apostle Peter performed washings and anointings as well as other ordinances in a "house" of God or temple (ibid., 211, 213).

8. See *Ensign,* February 1995, 2; Victor L. Ludlow, *Principles and Practices of the Restored Gospel* (Salt Lake City: Deseret Book, 1992), 348.

9. *EM,* 3:1342.

10. Ibid., 4:1444.

11. Ibid., 2:534.

12. Ibid., 1:399.

13. Ibid., 4:1445.

14. Ibid., 3:1138.

15. "How are [the Saints] to become saviors on Mount Zion? By building their temples, erecting their baptismal fonts, and going forth and receiving all the ordinances, baptisms, confirmations, washings, anointings, ordinations and sealing powers upon their heads, in behalf of all their progenitors who are dead, and redeem them that they may come forth in the first resurrection and be exalted to thrones of glory with them; and herein is the chain that binds the hearts of the fathers to the children, and the children to the fathers" (Brigham H. Roberts, ed., *History of the Church* [Salt Lake City: Deseret News Press, 1930], 6:184; hereafter cited as *HC*).

16. See *EM,* 3:1288.

17. See *HC,* 6:251–52. Joseph Smith said that the sealing power of God's priesthood would enable a person to enter the presence of Deity (see *WJS,* 246) and he connected such an ability and privilege with temple ordinances of the "holy order" (see JST, Ex. 34:1–2).

18. *Ensign,* May 2006, 67.

19. *EM,* 3:1257.

20. Bruce R. McConkie, *Mormon Doctrine* (Salt Lake City: Bookcraft, 1966), 227.

21. *HC,* 6:319.

22. Ezra Taft Benson, *The Teachings of Ezra Taft Benson* (Salt Lake City: Bookcraft, 1988), 250.

23. United Grand Lodge of England website, link path (all such links as of July 2009): All about Masonry, What is Freemasonry? Introduction and Freemasonry and Religion.

24. See Albert G. Mackey, *An Encylopaedia of Freemasonry,* rev. ed. (New York: The Masonic History Company, 1921), 1:449; Robert L. D. Cooper, *Cracking the Freemasons Code* (New

York: Atria Books, 2006), 14; Herbert Applebaum, *The Concept of Work* (New York: State University of New York Press, 1992), 281; S. Brent Morris, *The Complete Idiot's Guide to Freemasonry* (New York: Alpha Books, 2006), 11.

25. Mackey, *An Encyclopaedia of Freemasonry*, 1:200.

26. United Grand Lodge of England website, link path: All about Masonry, What is Freemasonry? The Essential Qualification for Membership.

27. Freemasons Hall in London can be hired for a wide variety of events including filming, conferences, dances, product launches, fashion shows, and dinners. A note on the website of the United Grand Lodge of England states that Freemasons Hall is "fully open to the public" (United Grand Lodge of England website, link path: News and Events, Events and Room Hire).

28. Mackey, *An Encyclopaedia of Freemasonry*, 1:290. Masonic author Walter Wilmhurst wrote that certain initiatic portions of Freemasonry must also be understood on a non-literal level. "In Masonry [the] prototype is Hiram Abiff: but it must be made clear that there is no historical basis whatever for the legendary account of Hiram's death. The entire story is symbolical and was purposely invented for the symbolical purposes of [Masonic] teaching" (Walter L. Wilmhurst, *The Meaning of Masonry: The Deeper Symbolism of Freemasonry* [Whitefish, MT: Kessinger Publishing, 1995], 44).

29. United Grand Lodge of England website, link path: All about Masonry, What is Freemasonry? Introduction.

30. United Grand Lodge of England website, link path: All about Masonry, Your Questions Answered, About Freemasonry, What is Freemasonry?

31. See Mackey, *An Encyclopaedia of Freemasonry*, 1:51, 70–71, 72–73, 173–74, 261–62, 290, 442–43, 2:474–75, 551, 570–71, 708–709, 804, 811; Henry W. Coil, *Coil's Masonic Encyclopedia* (New York: Macoy Publishing and Masonic Supply Company, 1961), 306.

32. United Grand Lodge of England website, link path: All about Masonry, What is Freemasonry? The Three Great Principles.

33. Eric Ward, "The Birth of Free-Masonry: The Creation of a Myth," *Ars Quatuor Coronatorum*, vol. 91, 1978, 77–86.

34. See Morris, *The Complete Idiot's Guide to Freemasonry*, 1, 13.

35. See ibid., 11–12.

36. See Albert G. Mackey, *The Symbolism of Freemasonry* (New York: Clark and Maynard, 1869), 147–58.

37. There are a great many elements in the first three Masonic initiation ceremonies that have no connection whatever to Mormon ordinances. Elements of this type which can be found in Masonic publications from the time of Joseph Smith include: officers who are present during ceremonies (master, wardens, deacons, treasurer, secretary), three candles/lights, circumambulation, emphasis on cardinal directions, call from labor to refreshment, the Great Architect of the Universe, opening and closing prayer, business proceedings, balloting for candidates, blindfold, cable-tow/rope, space is called a lodge, the holy lodge of St. John at Jerusalem, candidate declares trust in God, sharp object being pressed against candidate's body, reading of a Psalm, ritualized walking steps, touching of the Bible to take an oath, mention of the parts, points, and secret arts of Freemasonry, clapping of hands/"the shock," stamping the floor, pillars Jachin and Boaz, Solomon's temple, different ways of wearing an apron, working tools of a mason (twenty-four-inch gauge, gavel, trowel), jewels, check-words, divested of all metals, candidate asked to give a metallic memorial, ritualized method of standing, motion given for closing the lodge, asking if the assembly is satisfied with proceedings, entire lecture of each degree in Q&A format, placement of legs and feet in a symbolic shape, clothing configuration that signifies distress/destitution, the teaching that the left side is the weakest part of the

body, the ancient pagan deity called Fides, the apron represents innocence, cornerstone placement in the northeast, mention of a charter that enables work to be performed, wisdom-beauty-strength, Jacob's ladder, faith-hope-charity, ornaments/checkered pavement-indented tessels-blazing star, Bethlehem, trestle board, rough ashlar, perfect ashlar, churches and chapels, Moses and the Red Sea, King Solomon as an ancient Grand Master, St. John the Evangelist and St. John the Baptist, politics, the value of two cents and one cent, swearing to support the constitution of the Grand Lodge, the valley of Jehosaphat, Succoth and Zaradatha, changing configuration of mason tools, kissing the scriptures, lettering or syllabling words, symbol-filled floor carpet, mention of speculative activity, maps of the heavens and the earth, mythological material on the pillars of Solomon's Temple serving as archives, the winding staircase in Solomon's Temple, five orders of architecture, the five human senses, seven sabbatical years, seven years of famine, seven years in building Solomon's Temple, seven golden candlesticks in Solomon's Temple, seven planets, seven wonders of the world, seven liberal arts and sciences, Jeptha and the Ephraimites, army-war-battle, the river Jordan, the letter "G" denoting Deity, the destruction of Solomon's Temple, emphasis on geometry (and claiming geometry and Masonry were originally synonymous), Grand Master Hiram Abiff, corn and the waterford, charge to conceal another initiate's secrets, no help for the widow's son, humanity-friendship-brotherly love, so mote it be, white gloves, three ruffians, physical assault with weapons, enactment of a murder, coast of Joppa, Ethiopia, buried in the rough sands of the sea at low watermark, kingly court/judgment scene, execution of murderers, discovery of a grave, substitute word, faint letter "G" on the chest, raising of a dead body from a grave, the "traditional accounts"/Old Charges, the drawing of architectural plans and designs, a sprig of acacia/the immortal soul, a cavern in the cleft of a rock, a coffin, being buried for two weeks, monument of a weeping virgin and broken column, an urn with ashes, a depiction of Time, no rain for seven years in the daytime while the temple was being built, thousands of pillars and columns made of Parian marble to support the temple of Solomon, the king of Tyre, a pot of incense, the beehive, a book of constitutions, Tiler's sword, heart, anchor, all-seeing eye, Noah's ark, 47th problem of Euclid, hourglass, scythe, Pythagoras, Eureka, Greek language, sacrifice of a hecatomb, three stairs/three stages of life/Entered Apprentice-Fellowcraft-Master Mason, a spade, a death-head, and due-guards.

CHAPTER 2

From Stonemasons to Freemasons

In order to gain the most accurate understanding of the connection between the Prophet Joseph Smith and the Masonic fraternity, it is necessary to answer two simple (but ultimately very different) questions: "Where did the Freemasons come from?" and "Where did the practices of the Freemasons come from?" The first question will be examined in this chapter, with the second question being addressed in the next chapter.

Masonic history is very problematic for historians.[1] There are multiple reasons for this. To begin with, the first known attempt at scribing the history of the Masons took place during the transition period of the fourteenth and fifteenth centuries AD, and it is admitted by Masonic historians that the earliest relevant document about Masonry contains various "extravagances and improbabilities."[2] The next earliest Masonic document was written not long thereafter and together they form the basis of a class of Masonry-related texts that have come to be known as the Old Charges or Gothic Constitutions. The information that is found in these manuscripts must be evaluated with care. One modern commentator on these medieval writings has said straightforwardly that

> though the Old Charges are basically similar to other craft histories, they are unusually elaborate. . . . If studied in search of the historical truth about the origins of the mason craft, the Old Charges may be dismissed as rubbish, impressive exercises in the dubious skills of name-dropping and creative chronology.[3]

Unfortunately, the documentary problem did not end with these texts from the Middle Ages. In September 1721, shortly after the Grand Lodge in England began to govern speculative (or non-operative, theoretical) Freemasons, it was realized that the Old Charges contained "many false facts and gross errors of history and chronology." A speculative Mason by the name of James Anderson was given the job of digesting them all "in a new and better method," thereby creating updated Constitutions for the Craft. The situation was not rectified by this action, however. One respected specialist on Masonic history—who is sympathetic to James Anderson—has candidly written that "taken as history as judged by modern scholarly standards, Anderson's account is clearly absurd." This writer even goes so far as to specify that the Book of Constitutions' "history of Masonry is worthless" from an academic standpoint. But it needs to be remembered that this speculative Masonic production "reflects conventional historical concepts of [Anderson's] age applied to a specialist account of the Masonic past." The problem is that the unreliable history of the Book of Constitutions was given official approval by the Grand Lodge in London and the tales within it were perpetuated as if they were history for a very long time (nine editions of the volume were printed by 1841).[4]

In 1884, a group of Freemasons got together in London, England, and started challenging the accuracy of what they termed the "romantic school" of Masonic history. They labeled their own views the "authentic school" because they insisted on applying the canons of historical research to what took place in Freemasonry's past.[5] This change in approach has improved segments of Masonic scholarship to a great degree. Yet, there are still those who persist in hanging on to mythological ideas about how Freemasonry was instituted and how it evolved over time.

EXISTING PROPOSITIONS

The question of the origin of the Freemasons is a straightforward enough query, and yet—as demonstrated previously—arriving at a clear-cut answer is much more difficult than one might suppose. "The precise origins of Freemasonry are unknown, and may perhaps remain so," reports a volume produced by some of the most respected of modern Masonic scholars. And they further inform their readership that the traditional history of Masonry enshrined in the fraternity's eighteenth-century Constitutions (which claimed Masonic descent from the biblical patriarchs and King Solomon's Temple) is "romantic and wholly fictitious"—none of it has "the slightest basis in truth," they say. Indeed, they note that such ideas were "discreetly dropped" from Freemasonry's Constitutions back in the year 1815.[6]

Though the traditional viewpoint of Masonic origins is in the most serious jeopardy, there are still some Freemasons, and outsiders alike, who staunchly adhere to it.[7] But it must be made clear that this is not the only belief that is held about Masonry's origination. Indeed, according to some other respected writers on this topic, "The mystery of Freemasonry's beginnings has provided a fertile field for both historical inquiry and some outright crackpot speculations."[8] Some of the more popular propositions of origin have included connections with the pyramid builders of Egypt, the people who constructed Stonehenge, the Italian Comacines, and the more ancient Collegia Fabrorum of Rome.[9] There are two other theories that need to be mentioned here because of their persistence in the public consciousness. The first is the Rosicrucian hypothesis. The Rosicrucians were first mentioned, anonymously, in print in AD 1614, but their very existence as an actual brotherhood has been called into question. It must be acknowledged that "supporters of the Rosicrucian theory of origin [for Freemasonry] have been consistently unable to bring forward any corroborative historical evidence for their belief."[10] The second theory regards the Knights Templar, a Roman Catholic monastic order set up in AD 1118 as a way to supply guards for persons making pilgrimages to various sites in Jerusalem. While the most careful Masonic historians admit that there are "superficial similarities" between the Templar and Masonic organizations, they conclude from the preponderance of evidence that the concept of Templars in hiding who eventually resurfaced as Freemasons "is not supported by the historical record" and "has no foundations in fact whatsoever."[11]

Where does all of this leave the student of the past? Empty-handed. There seems to be no solid consensus on where the Masonic organization and its rituals came from. Even after the Masonic historians themselves offer up what they feel to be a plausible theory of indirect descent, they are left to lament, "How, when, and why Freemasonry arose are still questions to which we have no final answers."[12]

CONTINUING THE SEARCH

Since an accurate understanding of the nature of Freemasonry cannot be obtained without an accurate understanding of the origin of Freemasonry, it is imperative that serious researchers in this field attempt to separate the myths from the facts. The investigation of this topic must be centered on historically verifi-able realities and not on romantic notions and legendary tales. The best way to approach this problematic issue is, perhaps, to begin by arranging indisputable ideas along a timeline and then evaluating them both individually and collectively.

One thing that is known for certain about the nature of Freemasonry is that it has a pronounced connection with the craft of the stonemasons. And this is where the first distinction needs to be made. The Freemasonry of today is a speculative, instead of an operative institution. The operative masons were stone cutters, stone shapers, and stone setters. The specula-tive Freemasons, on the other hand, do not engage in any such physical activities but are concerned with integrating a system of ethics into their lives. Still,

> there is undoubtedly a connection between medieval operative masons and what we now

call speculative Freemasonry: the very structure of the Craft makes this clear. But the exact
nature of the connection remains uncertain and
scholars continue to dispute the question, with
some arguing for a direct descent from operative
masonry, and others for a more complex, indirect
link.[13]

It is the operative side of this equation that must be the
starting point for adequately understanding the story of the
Freemasons. And since it is known that speculative Freemasonry
formed into a coherent system in the British Isles, it is only
logical to start a research timeline in that locality. It was in AD
1356 that trade regulations were established for operative stonemasons at Guildhall in London, England.[14] It is believed that
sometime between 1356 and 1376, the first trade guild of stonemasons was formed in the same location.[15] About fifty years after
this, something very significant occurred. Dr. Andrew Prescott—
former director of the Center for Research into Freemasonry and
Fraternalism at the University of Sheffield—writes,

> In 1425, [in England] a statute was passed forbid-
> ding holding assemblies to demand higher wages.
> It is in this event that we can find the beginnings
> of the myths of Freemasonry. Groups of junior
> masons developed a legend that they had been
> given ancient charters allowing them to hold
> their assemblies. They also reacted against the
> increasing stratification of their trade by devel-
> oping legends which sought to demonstrate that
> all masons were brethren of equal status. The two
> manuscripts recording these legends, preserved in
> the British Library and known as the Regius and
> Cooke manuscripts, were apparently used by these
> illicit gatherings [of stoneworkers]. . . . [T]he evident
> manipulation of these legends in [the] Regius and

Cooke [documents] indicates that the legends were in 1425 of recent invention and primarily intended to protect stonemasons from the effects of recent labor legislation.[16]

The two manuscripts that are mentioned here are of primary importance in the history of Freemasonry because they are the earliest available documents that pertain specifically to what eventually became the institution of speculative Freemasons. Of the two documents, the Regius manuscript appears to be the earliest one produced, about AD 1425–50. The Cooke text was probably written sometime around 1450.[17] Masonic researcher Douglas Hamer believed that the Regius text was written by an Augustinian canon at Lantony Priory near Gloucester, England.[18] It was written in poetic form and had a very strong Roman Catholic influence manifested throughout.[19] This is an important thing to keep in mind as one confronts the double issues of where Freemasonry came from and where the practices of Freemasonry originated. All of the Old Charges up until AD 1717 "are specifically Christian, so far as religion is concerned."[20] And "common to the majority of the Old Charges is the linking of biblical characters with the craft of the masons" as well as Bible traditions and Old Testament legends.[21] It is in the Cooke document that a connection is made between stonemasons and the building of King Solomon's Temple.

A close study of the Regius and Cooke manuscripts shows that the rudimentary elements of later Masonic initiation rites can be detected within them, but it must be remembered that in the fifteenth century there was only one initiation process for all stonemasons in the trade, consisting of not much more than gaining legend-based knowledge, learning lessons about moral or ethical behavior, and swearing an oath to adhere to the charges of the worker's association.[22]

Next on the timeline is 1475. During this year, the stonemasons and the wrights (carpenters) were incorporated together in Edinburgh, Scotland.[23] The close association between these two Scottish trades became pertinent in an interesting way. The woodworkers had a natural attachment to Noah from the Bible and one of the surviving Old Charges from 1726 (which may be Scottish in origin) contains legends about Noah and his sons that were eventually worked into the ritualism of the Masonic initiation ceremonies.

As noted previously, the English stonemasons had legendary material associated with their craft in the documents known as the Old Charges or Gothic Constitutions. These texts also contained information that was connected with being initiated into the group of operative stonemasons. But the ceremonies were of simple content, were grounded in orthodox Christian practice, and were only faint echoes of those activities and themes that would later characterize speculative Freemasonry. It was not so among the operative stonemasons of Scotland, however. They had among themselves something known as the "Mason Word." It consisted of certain esoteric matters and was established among the Scottish stonemasons sometime before AD 1550.[24] Masonic writer Harry Carr states that it is generally agreed among the historians of Masonry that the "Mason Word" was "probably of Hebrew origin."[25]

On 21 December 1583, William Schaw was appointed as the Master of Works for Scotland under King James VI. Only two days later, a Masonic document known as Grand Lodge Manuscript #1 was created—possibly for Schaw himself. This document contained the same legendary material that was recorded in the Regius and Cooke manuscripts.[26] An important evolutionary step in Freemasonry is first recorded in the minutes of Aitchison's Haven lodge near Edinburgh, Scotland. On 9 January 1598, two separate degrees were noted: those of "entered prentice" and "fellow of craft."[27] On the 28th of December in 1598 and 1599, William Schaw issued what are now known as the first and second Schaw Statutes, which regulated the operative stonemasons of the entire Scottish realm. Professor David Stevenson of Aberdeen University in Scotland has published the opinion that William Schaw "gave the masons a lodge system . . . as well as its esoteric rituals; and it is highly probable," he says, "that these rituals themselves and the values and beliefs they enshrined also owed much to Schaw."[28] This idea becomes much more interesting when one realizes that William Schaw was Roman Catholic by religious profession,[29] and this was the time of the Reformation in the British Isles. Masonic writer Robert Gilbert has theorized that perhaps Freemasonry's ritual system ultimately "sought to construct a secular substitute for the elaborate Catholic liturgy that was lost at the time of the Reformation."[30] This viewpoint will receive a substantial amount of support in the next chapter of the present volume.

On 3 July 1634, men who were not operative stonemasons were initiated into a Mason's lodge in Edinburgh, Scotland. Other non-operatives were admitted to the same lodge between 1635 and 1638.[31] The reason for the association of these men with the lodges of the operatives is unclear, but it could have been for the sake of curiosity about the organization's teachings, supplying patronage, or honorary affiliation.[32] Thus, Masonic lodges began another transitional phase.

On 20 May 1641, Sir Robert Moray (a Scottish non-operative and one of the founding members of the Royal Society) was initiated on English soil (Newcastle) by several members of the Mary's Chapel Lodge of Edinburgh, Scotland. This was the first known non-operative Masonic initiation in England, but it was the initiation of a Scot into a Scottish system.[33]

Elias Ashmole (another member of the Royal Society and an English non-operative) was initiated as a Freemason on 16 October 1646 in Warrington, Lancashire, England. The temporary "lodge" that did the initiating consisted of all non-operatives.[34]

Now that it has been shown that the mixture of Scottish and English Freemasonry had begun at this general time period, it is of interest to note that some Masonic scholars believe that around AD 1650, the legendary material in the Old Charges or Gothic Constitutions of England was combined with the esoteric Mason Word material of Scotland to form the basis of speculative Freemasonry.[35] Indeed, it was in 1672 that the earliest known published mention of "the Mason's word" (a distinctive Scottish term) appeared in England.[36]

On 24 June 1717 (St. John's Day, a religious festival)—a landmark day in the history of Freemasonry—four lodges of completely non-operative Masons met in London, England, to form a Grand Lodge. This organization did not become a regulatory body until 1721, however.[37]

In 1721, James Anderson, a Scottish Presbyterian minister,[38] was assigned by the Grand Lodge of London to write a book that digested and refashioned information ("in a new and better method") from the Old Charges of the operative stonemasons. This volume was published in 1723 and was entitled *The Constitutions of the Freemasons, Containing the History, Charges, Regulations, etc. of that Most Ancient and Right Worshipful Fraternity.*[39]

A major development took place among the Masons in the year 1725. It was at this time that the two degrees of initiation in Freemasonry were expanded into three: Entered Apprentice, Fellow Craft, and Master Mason.[40] It is important to remember that all three degrees went through various stages of metamorphosis after they were first established.[41]

There was dissension in 1751 among the Free and Accepted Masons of England. In July of that year, a group of speculative Irish Freemasons met in London and formed a rival governing body, labeling it The Grand Lodge of England According to the Old Institutions. They called themselves the "Ancients" and referred to the first London Grand Lodge as the "Moderns," because the Irishmen accused them of changing the ancient landmarks of Masonry. This rift continued for sixty-three years.[42]

Between 1809 and 1813, the two opposing Grand Lodges negotiated with each other for reconciliation. An agreement was reached and the groups finally integrated on 27 December 1813 as the United Grand Lodge of England under the leadership of His Royal Highness the Duke of Sussex.[43] Just a few days before the English Freemasons united their numbers and began the process of streamlining the ways they conducted initiation ceremonies, Joseph Smith Jr. turned eight years old in the United States.

NOTES

1. After summarizing ten competing theories of Masonic origins proposed by Freemasons themselves, one scholar of the organization reports, "As the twentieth century ends, the origins of speculative Masonry still remain shrouded in mystery" (Roeinton B. Khambatta, "Ars Quatuor Coronatorum of the Twentieth Century," *Ars Quatuor Coronatorum*, vol. 114, 2001, 1–9).

2. Harry L. Haywood and James E. Craig, *History of Freemasonry* (Whitefish, MT: Kessinger Publishing, 2003), 8–9.

3. David Stevenson, *The Origins of Freemasonry: Scotland's Century 1590–1710*, rev. ed. (New York: Cambridge University Press, 1988), 23–24.

4. Henry L. Stillson, ed., *History of the Ancient and Honorable Fraternity of Free and Accepted Masons* (Boston: The Fraternity Publishing Company, 1892), 545; David Stevenson, "James Anderson: Man and Mason," *Heredom*, vol. 10, 2002, 110, 113; Albert G. Mackey, *An Encyclopaedia of Freemasonry*, rev. ed. (New York: The Masonic History Company, 1921), 1:112–13.

5. S. Brent Morris, *The Complete Idiot's Guide to Freemasonry* (New York: Alpha Books, 2006), 130.

6. John Hamill and Robert Gilbert, eds., *Freemasonry: A Celebration of the Craft* (London: Mackenzie Publishing, 1992), 13–14.

7. Masonic author Harry Carr noted, "I travel vast distances in the course of my lecture duties and the further I go the more astonished I am to see how many Brethren believe, quite genuinely, that our Masonic ritual came down straight from heaven, directly into the hands of King Solomon. They are all quite certain that it was in English, of course, because that is the only language they speak up there. They are equally sure that it was all engraved on two tablets of stone, so that, heaven forbid, not one single word should ever be altered; and most of them believe that King Solomon, in his own lodge, practiced the same ritual

as they do in theirs. But, it was not like that at all" (Harry Carr, "600 Years of Craft Ritual," *Ars Quatuor Coronatorum*, vol. 81, 1968, 153).

8. Arturo de Hoyos and S. Brent Morris, eds., *Freemasonry in Context: History, Ritual, Controversy* (Lanham, MD: Lexington Books, 2004), 1.

9. Hamill and Gilbert, eds., *Freemasonry: A Celebration of the Craft*, 14.

10. Ibid., 20. Despite the fact that there is no proven direct link between the Rosicrucians and the Freemasons, there is some historical information that is of great interest. Consider the following: the Rosicrucian ideology championed a religious reformation; the story of "Christian Rosenkreutz" (Rosenkreutz meaning "Rose Cross") had similarities to the life of Jesus Christ and utilized allegory; the Rosicrucian Order was depicted as the "Protestant equivalent of a medieval monastic order"; the apparent author of the Rosicrucian Manifestos was a Lutheran theologian from Germany (ibid.). The connection between Lutheranism and the Rose Cross lies in the fact that the seal of German reformer Martin Luther consisted of a combination of Jesus Christ's cross and a rose (Letter, 8 July 1530, Martin Luther to Lazarus Spengler in Gottfried G. Krodel and Helmut T. Lehmann, eds., *Luther's Works* (Philadelphia: Fortress Press, 1972), 49:358–59). Now consider the fact that in 1638, a publication in Edinburgh, Scotland, said that the "brethren of the Rosie Crosse" possessed "the Mason word," (Henry Adamson, *The Muses' Threnodie*, third muse, para. 5, lines 200–201). Since, as noted in the main body of the present chapter, the stone-masons of Scotland also had the "Mason Word" one senses a possible line of transmittal for the "Mason Word" from a religious source to a secular organization which had strong religious affiliations.

11. Hamill and Gilbert, eds., *Freemasonry: A Celebration of the Craft*, 17–18.

12. Ibid., 25.

13. Ibid., 14.

14. See Douglas D. Knoop and Gwilym P. Jones, *The Mediaeval Mason: An Economic History of English Stone Building in the Later Middle Ages and Early Modern Times* (Manchester: University of Manchester Press, 1933), 151–52.

15. See ibid., 152.

16. Andrew Prescott, "A History of British Freemasonry 1425–2000," Working Papers Series No. 1, 20 February 2007, The Centre for Research into Freemasonry and Fraternalism at the University of Sheffield, 8–9.

17. Andrew Prescott, "The Old Charges Revisited," *Transactions of the Lodge of Research No. 2429* (Leicester, Lodge of Research No. 2429, 2006), para. 8. For a more detailed examination of the question of dating for the Regius and Cooke manuscripts see Andrew Prescott, "Some Literary Contexts of the Regius and Cooke Manuscripts," in Trevor Stewart, ed., *Freemasonry in Music and Literature* (London: Canonbury Masonic Research Centre, 2005), 1–36.

18. See Douglas Hamer, "Further Consideration of the Regius MS," *Ars Quatuor Coronatorum,* vol. 94, 1981, 166–68.

19. See Albert G. Mackey, *The History of Freemasonry: Its Legendary Origins* (New York: Gramercy Books, 1996), 30–32.

20. *The Builder Magazine,* vol. 9, no. 9, September 1923, para. 12.

21. Roy A. Wells, "The Structure of Freemasonry," para. 14, Grand Lodge of Scotland website, link path: Masonic Subjects, Masonic Articles, The Structure of Freemasonry.

22. For published, modern English renditions of the Regius and Cooke manuscripts see Henry L. Stillson and William J. Hughan, *History of the Ancient and Honorable Fraternity of Free and Accepted Masons and Concordant Orders,* rev. ed. (New York: Fraternity Publishing Company, 1902), 164–85.

23. See Robert L. D. Cooper, *Cracking the Freemasons Code*

(New York: Atria Books, 2006), 11–12.

24. Douglas D. Knoop and Gwilym P. Jones, *The Genesis of Freemasonry* (London: Q. C. Correspondence Circle, 1978), 105.

25. Harry Carr, *The Freemason at Work*, 6th ed. (London: Lewis Masonic, 1981), 9.

26. See Andrew Prescott, "A History of British Freemasonry 1425–2000," Working Papers Series No. 1, 20 February 2007, The Centre for Research into Freemasonry and Fraternalism at the University of Sheffield, 10.

27. See Carr, *The Freemason at Work*, 373.

28. David Stevenson, *The Origins of Freemasonry: Scotland's Century, 1590–1710*, rev. ed. (Cambridge: Cambridge University Press, 1990), 76. Professor Stevenson believes that William Schaw grafted late Renaissance themes onto the traditional lore of the Old Charges and thereby created "a new type of Masonic lodge" for the operative stonemasons of Scotland (ibid., 228, 232–33). Masonic author W. Kirk MacNulty thinks that instead of trying to establish a direct link between the Freemasons and the initiation rites of the classical period of history "it is more reasonable to understand that Masonic ideas were derived from the revival of antiquity in the Renaissance" time frame (W. Kirk MacNulty, *Freemasonry: Symbols, Secrets, Significance* [New York: Thames and Hudson, 2006], 53).

29. See H. C. G. Matthew and Brian Harrison, eds., *Oxford Dictionary of National Biography* (New York: Oxford University Press, 2004), 206.

30. Robert A. Gilbert, "Freemasonry and Esoteric Movements," Canonbury Masonic Research Center, lecture, 1 March 2000, para. 8.

31. Stevenson, *The Origins of Freemasonry: Scotland's Century, 1590–1710*, 198.

32. See De Hoyos and Morris, eds., *Freemasonry in Context: History, Ritual, Controversy*, 4.

33. See Stillson, ed., *History of the Ancient and Honorable Fraternity of Free and Accepted Masons*, xxiv; *Renaissance Quarterly*, vol. 60, no. 4, Winter 2007, 1446.

34. See Joseph F. Newton, *Modern Masonry: A Brief Sketch of the Craft since 1717* (Washington, D.C.: The Masonic Service Association of the United States, 1924), 5.

35. Knoop and Jones, *The Genesis of Freemasonry*, 216–18.

36. Alexander B. Grosart, ed., *The Complete Works of Andrew Marvell* (New York: AMS Press, 1966), 3:55.

37. See Mackey, *An Encyclopaedia of Freemasonry*, 2:622–23, 659; Morris, *A Complete Idiot's Guide to Freemasonry*, 9; De Hoyos and Morris, eds., *Freemasonry in Context: History, Ritual, Controversy*, 12.

38. See Robert F. Gould, *The History of Freemasonry: Its Antiquities, Symbols, Constitutions, Customs, Etc.* (London: Thomas C. Jack, 1885), 4:292–93.

39. Mackey, *An Encyclopaedia of Freemasonry*, 1:112.

40. J. A. M. Snoek, "On the Creation of Masonic Degrees: A Method and Its Fruits" in Antoine Faivre and Wouter J. Hanegraff, eds., *Western Esotericism and the Science of Religion* (Leuven: Peeters, 1998), 147–50.

41. The branchlike development of Masonic ideology and ritual from the 1700s onward is a complex issue and is beyond the scope of this volume. For a general overview of such things see William J. Hamblin and David R. Seely, *Solomon's Temple: Myth and History* (New York: Thames and Hudson, 2007), 182–86; Margaret C. Jacob, *Living the Enlightenment: Freemasonry and Politics in Eighteenth-Century Europe* (New York: Oxford University Press, 1991).

42. Robert F. Gould, *The Concise History of Freemasonry* (Whitefish, MT: Kessinger Publishing, 1994), 252.

43. See Robert F. Gould, *The Four Old Lodges: Founders of Modern Freemasonry and Their Descendants* (London: Spencer's Masonic Depot, 1879), 36.

CHAPTER 3

The Origins of
Masonic Practice

In the previous chapter, it was proposed that in order to properly understand the connection between the Prophet Joseph Smith and the institution of Freemasonry, two questions need to be answered: "Where did the Freemasons come from?" and "Where did the practices of the Freemasons come from?" The present chapter will address the second question and in the process offer a plausible answer to the long-standing question of Masonic ritual beginnings.

"Will we ever find the origins of Freemasonry?" asks John Hamill, the director of communications for the United Grand Lodge of England. He admits that he can provide no positive answer to that interrogatory, but he asks another pointed question that all researchers on this topic need to carefully consider: "Have we, in fact, been looking in the wrong places for evidence of early Freemasonry?" And then he poses the most important question of all to his fellow Masons: "Do we actually want to find out our origins?"[1]

The medieval documents associated with the operative stonemasons provide the greatest clue about the origin and nature of Freemasonry's beliefs and practices. Masonic authors Fred L. Pick and G. Norman Knight have written that "the Old Charges have almost without exception a positively Christian character."[2] This is clear from a perusal of the earliest of these documents known as the Regius Poem and the Cooke Manuscript. There the operative masons are warned not to swear false oaths for dread of their soul's sake, are admonished to go to church and observe proper etiquette while they are there, to "love well God and holy church," to "stand well in God's law," and to pray. Reference is made to the "book" or Bible and to several of the stories that are contained therein. Christian martyrs and finding a place in heaven's bliss are also mentioned.[3]

Orthodox Christianity is the place to start looking when it comes to the question of Masonic origins. The *Encyclopedia Britannica* goes so far as to state that up "until the Grand Lodge era [of AD 1717], Freemasonry was . . . wholly Christian" in nature.[4] Robert Cooper—the Curator of the Grand Lodge of Scotland Museum and Library—puts it plainly: "Freemasonry adopted much Christian symbolism and iconography. . . . Freemasonry doubtless used other sources and invented some, but the majority were adopted from Christianity."[5] How far did the borrowing of the Masons extend? According to John Hamill, "None of the symbolism employed in Freemasonry is peculiar to Freemasonry. It has all been borrowed."[6] With this perspective in mind, it seems prudent to look at orthodox Christianity as a source for the setting and practices of the Freemasons.

MASONIC LODGES IMITATE CHRISTIAN CHURCHES

The three basic initiation degrees of Freemasonry are carried out against the allegorical backdrop of King Solomon's Temple. The candidate is figuratively taken through the three areas of the biblical sanctuary complex as they progress and encounter symbolic representations of that temple's exterior pillars and interior staircase to reinforce a sense of connection with that building. Because of this strong mental, visual, and ritual link to the ancient Hebrew structure, the Masonic lodge is automatically associated in the minds of Masons and non-Masons alike with the idea of a temple. But there are other pieces of lodge ornament and furniture, and also designation, that point to another ecclesiastical connection—one that cannot be overlooked in the quest to identify the sources of Masonic practice.

The English word *lodges* comes from the Anglo-Saxon *logian* which means 'to dwell.' Some people are of the belief that "in the Middle Ages *logia* or *logium* was commonly used for an apartment or dwelling connected with [a] main building. Thus, the smallest apartments occupied by the cardinals when meeting in conclave were called *logiae* or Lodges."[7]

The first item of ornament to be noted is the mosaic floor pavement of alternating black-and-white squares. The tradition of the Freemasons is that this was the design found on the ground floor of King Solomon's Temple, emblematic of the good and evil of human life.[8] Masonic historians are clear in stating that this tradition is not accurate but relies on "a little torsion of historical accuracy."[9] The idea comes from Samuel Lee's imaginative 1659 drawings of the Solomonic Temple.[10] The Masonic notion and its accompanying imagery first showed up in sources in 1730 and 1744.[11] There are a number of ecclesiastical Christian buildings predating the formal organization of Freemasonry that were equipped with a pavement of black-and-white squares—the choir section of Westminster Abbey (ca. AD 1690) is one such example.[12] One Masonic researcher writes that "according to some very old books and pictures (especially one by Holbein), the black and white–checkered pavement when laid in a church or cathedral symbolized the eternity of the world, in contrast to which a man, as he walked across the earth, was very humble and very transient."[13]

The next piece of Masonic furniture that has an obvious connection to ancient Christian churches is the altar. The lodges of York Rite Masonry contain only one altar, and it is placed in the center of the room. Masonic historian Albert G. Mackey calls this "the most important article of furniture in a lodge room." He says that even though this item is of a "symbolic" nature, it is "not merely a convenient article of furniture intended, like a table, to hold a Bible." Mackey asserts that "it is a sacred utensil of religion intended, like the altars of the ancient temples, for religious uses." He further states that the Masonic altar identifies the organization "as a religious institution."[14] The Masons place an open volume of sacred law (dependant on the faith of the initiate) on their lodge altars along with architectural tools. In comparison, as early as AD 847–855, Christians had formal guidelines regarding the placement of the book of Gospels and Saintly relics on the top of their church altars.[15]

At three sides of the Masonic altar sit three tall candlesticks. They are known collectively as the Lesser Lights of the lodge. Their connection to medieval Christian churches—and especially to the altar of those churches—is immediately apparent. The *Catholic Encyclopedia* states that "no writer before the tenth century [AD] who [discusses] the altar makes mention of candlesticks on the altar, but mention is made of acolytes carrying candlesticks which, however, were placed on the floor of the sanctuary or near the corners of the altar, as [was] still the custom [at the turn of the twentieth century] in the Eastern Church."[16]

Next are the three laterally-placed chairs located in the eastern end of the lodge room; the middle seat is for the Master of the lodge and the other two are for the Secretary and Treasurer. The chair of the Master is raised up on a platform with three steps, while the other two are on ground level. Masonic author Alex Horne points out that Christian altars "are almost universally approached by a series of three steps (which may perhaps have led to the analogous practice of placing the Master's Chair . . . on a platform with the same number of steps)."[17] In addition, a parallel can be seen between the three Masonic seats, with the center one raised, and the bishop's throne or cathedra in old churches, which had seats at either side for inferior clergy members. Some of the ancient bishops' thrones and church altars were ascended by three steps, some by five, and some by seven—all significant numbers in Masonic ritual.[18] Sets of three cathedra-affiliated seats, with the center one raised, are still in use among orthodox Christians.[19]

Finally, there is the shining letter G. Albert Mackey reports that this symbol represents both geometry and the Grand Architect of the Universe—which, in the nomenclature of the Freemasons, is a generic reference for God. He also states that "as in all Roman Catholic and in many Protestant churches the cross, engraved or sculpted in some prominent position, will be found as the expressive symbol of Christianity, so in every Masonic lodge, a letter G may be seen in the east" portion of the room over the Master's chair.[20] It might be added that some early Christian churches displayed an all-seeing eye of God "above the east apse" of the building,[21] and in the 1611 printing of the King James Bible (on the genealogy page for Adam and Eve), the word *GOD* is shown with rays of light emanating from it.[22]

With so many direct correspondences between orthodox Christian church buildings and Masonic lodges, it should come as no real surprise if one discovers that Freemasonry has also drawn heavily from orthodox Christianity in formulating its initiation ceremonies.

MASONIC CEREMONIES IMITATE CHRISTIAN RITES

Freemasons do not discuss or display their ceremonies in detail, in public, and there are some things connected therewith which they desire to keep confidential. The discussion that follows will endeavor to show appropriate deference to the Masonic institution by only describing Freemasonry's rites in outline form and by only drawing that material from long-established and well-respected Masonic sources.

An important clue about the origin of Masonry's rituals can be found in the writings of one Masonic historian from the late nineteenth century. He noted that in the year 1870, he traveled to Rome and witnessed the initiation or profession of a Benedictine monk at St. Paul's Basilica. Here is a description of what he witnessed:

At one point of the ceremony a black cloth was laid on the floor in front of the altar; on this the novitiate lay down and was covered with a black pall. . . . A large candle stood at his head and another at his feet. There the man lay in semblance of death. The abbot of the order celebrated Mass, which occupied about half an hour. At the end of this the deacon of the Mass came near to the prostrate figure and reading from a book in his hand, in Latin, some words which were to this effect: "Oh, thou that sleepest, arise to everlasting life." The man rose up and, if I remember right, received the sacrament. He then took his place amongst the brethren of the order, [receiving the Kiss of Peace from] each of them as he passed along. The proof that he [was] supposed to leave one state of existence and become a new individual [was] supplied by the fact that when I asked his name it was refused to me. I was told that henceforth he would be known [by another moniker]—his old name went with the former existence. It is the same with nuns. They all receive a new name and they also go through the semblance of death as a final ceremony of the order.[23]

Those who are familiar with the initiation rites of Freemasonry cannot fail to recognize the parallels between this orthodox Christian ritual and that used for the induction of speculative Masons. Indeed, the further back in time one looks, the closer the connection between masons and the Christian faith becomes.[24]

Another Masonic author who took an interest in this line of thought in modern times was a reverend by the name of Neville B. Cryer. "I think I know where we came from," he said.

"The real basis of Freemasonry . . . is Christian understanding,"
and the purpose of the rites is to place a man on a figurative
pilgrimage to God's heavenly temple.[25] He based this viewpoint
on what he learned after asking questions such as, "From whence
did we get our Masonic history, our signs and symbols, our use
of allegory, our forms and penalties of obligation, our passwords and types of recognition, our early types of catechism and
instruction, our clothing, and our titles for the various offices?"
The most important question in his mind was, "Have we uncov-
ered what was the overall and truly original source and means
by which such material came to be adopted?" Reverend Cryer's
studies led him to the conclusion that some of the legendary
material of the Craft came from a world history composed by a
Roman Catholic monk. In addition, he concluded that Masonic
signs originated with the set of gestures utilized by a few of the
orthodox monastic orders. He felt that the catechetical instruction of Masonry was rooted in the method of monastic worship
(i.e., the chanter and deacon statement and response routine
performed in the choir; the question-and-answer sessions held
between the Novice Master and novitiates). Reverend Cryer
suspected that the art of memory among Masons came from
the stoneworker guild participating in the Mystery Plays and
also from prayer forms practiced in the monasteries. Allegory
coupled with symbolism—according to Cryer—can be traced
to the monk known as the Venerable Bede, who wrote about the
Israelite temple (his works even became part of monastic curric-
ulum). Finally, Cryer thought that the Jesuit monks employed
symbols that the Freemasons had adopted. The reverend felt
that altogether this constituted the "true ceremonial origins" of
Freemasonry, and he invited further study into the question.[26]

The paragraphs that follow are designed to fortify the idea
that the three fundamental initiation rites of Freemasonry are
solidly grounded in, and very likely drew from, the initiation
ceremonies of the orthodox Christian church. Each section will

begin with a brief description of what occurs among the Masons followed by information pertaining to the initiation of new Christian converts, monks or priests, and kings.

TEMPLE

The location of the Masonic initiation ceremonies is a lodge that is also identified with the ancient Israelite temple. "The symbolism of speculative Freemasonry is . . . intimately connected with temple building and temple worship," says one writer. "Masonry has derived its temple symbolism, as it has almost all its symbolic ideas, from the Hebrew type, and thus makes the temple the symbol of a lodge."[27]

Some converts or catechumens to the early Christian faith were to be initiated in a church structure which was identified as a "temple."[28] This ideology is still in place in some orthodox denominations and applies to the place where couples are being married also.[29]

GUARD

Among the Masons the Tiler is the guard of the door of a lodge whose job it is to make sure that only duly qualified and invited individuals enter within its precincts.[30] While on duty, the Tiler uses a small, predetermined number of knocks on the lodge door in order to communicate with those who are conducting business inside.[31]

A very early Christian text called the Apostolic Constitutions says of the church building, "Let the door be watched, lest any unbeliever, or one not yet initiated, come in."[32] In the ancient Coptic church, sub-deacons were assigned as doorkeepers of the Lord's "temple."[33] And it is made clear in some documents that Christian initiates had to pass by the doorkeepers.[34] Ceremonial door knocking can be seen at the dedicatory services of some early Christian churches. For instance, in about AD 750 in the area of Spain and Gaul (but influenced by the Eastern orthodox liturgy), the bishop would strike the front door three times with his pastoral staff while all those present sang Psalm 24—an Old Testament temple entrance text set in question-and-answer format. This was followed by entry through the door. This rite is particularly interesting because it was part of a complex series of actions that treated the building as if it were a person who was being initiated: the building was symbolically washed, anointed, clothed in white, and then illuminated with fire. Hence, the door knocking ceremony was tied together directly with the initiation rites of early Christianity.[35]

THREE DEGREES

According to some Masonic commentators the "original system of speculative Masonry" consisted only of the first three degrees: Entered Apprentice, Fellow Craft, and Master Mason. The Royal Arch degree (which is said to "complete" the Master Mason degree) was not declared to be part of the original system of initiation until 1813.[36]

In early eastern orthodox Christianity some monks were known to have been divided into three progressive orders (novices, the lesser habit, and the great habit), and these grades were distinguished by the putting on of increasingly more elaborate clothing.[37] Priestly initiation ceremonies among the medieval Copts specifically referred to a progressive "degree" system.[38]

DRAMA

The dramatization of a legend is performed during the Master Mason's degree of initiation.[39]

Liturgical drama among the Roman Catholics can be traced to England in the tenth century. The priests would take on the roles of characters from the Bible. In the twelfth century in France, there was a drama called *Adam* that was acted out at the gate of the church. It dealt with the Fall from paradise and went on to depict prophets foretelling the advent of the Redeemer.[40]

MANNER OF PREPARATION

The candidate for each Masonic degree of initiation is prepared beforehand by being dressed in a certain symbolic manner. The configuration of dress is different for each degree.[41]

The Masonic preparation has "very remarkable coincidences" with the preparatory conditions that had to be met by Israelites before they could enter the courts of the Lord's temple. In the Talmud (Baracoth) it is decreed: "No man shall go into the temple with his staff, nor with shoes on his feet, nor with his outer garment, nor with money tied up in his purse."[42] Some medieval and later Christian kings had to have their clothing arranged in certain ways so that they could experience all of the initiation rites.[43] The same was true for late nineteenth-century catechumens of the eastern orthodox tradition.[44]

PRAYER

During the initiation rites of Freemasonry, the Masonic candidate kneels to pray at an altar but the prayer is spoken on his behalf.[45]

Prayer while kneeling was part of some recorded initiatory rites for ancient catechumens.[46] Prayer for the Christian king at his initiation can be found as early as AD 491.[47] A tenth-century text notes that the king offered prayer at the iconostasis doors of the church while he was being initiated.[48] And, of course, some Christian monks/priests prayed while kneeling at an altar during their induction rites.[49] It should be pointed out that some priestly initiates were accustomed to kneeling on both knees at the altar for purposes other than prayer while at other times they only knelt on one knee.[50]

DARKNESS AND LIGHT

The Masonic candidate is brought from a state of figurative darkness or ignorance to one of light.[51]

Initiation texts for the early Christian catechumens are replete with references to the person being illuminated by the things he experiences.[52] Regarding royalty: "On the night before the coronation, the [Christian] king's sleep acquired a symbolic significance as reflected in his ritual waking on the next morning." A procession originating at the cathedral went to the king's room where he lay on his bed in priestly clothing. The metropolitan approached him, "stretched out his hand and helped the king to rise."[53]

OATHS AND OBLIGATIONS

During the three basic initiation rites of speculative Freemasonry, the Masons take upon themselves varying obligations which have affirmative and negative clauses attached to them—"like that of the precepts of the Jewish law."[54]

Masonic historians hint that the methods whereby Masonic oaths are taken follow customs practiced in the ancient Roman Catholic church.[55] It is known that early Christian catechumens made covenants when they participated in their initiation ceremonies.[56]

Augustinian monks in about AD 1500 would—after the year of their novitiate—kneel near an altar and swear on the rule book of the order to live a life of obedience, chastity, and poverty.[57] Kneeling on one or both knees, either at or near an altar, was part of the ordination rites of some medieval monks.[58] A Christian king in England would go to the altar and place his hand on the "Evangelists" and then swear an oath that he would adhere to the coronation promises which he had just made. He would then kiss the book.[59]

MYSTERIES

The things learned by a Masonic initiate during the reception of degrees are known as "mysteries."[60] The Freemasons have "an obligatory promise of secrecy among their ceremonies."[61]

The initiation rites of the early Christians were frequently referred to as "mysteries."[62] One fourteenth-century initiatory text for monks indicates that at their profession they "took [an] oath to preserve the secrets of the chapter."[63]

CIRCUMAMBULATION

The Freemasons employ a rite of circumambulation (a ritualistic walking around in a circle) during the implementation of their initiation scheme.[64]

When a medieval Greek priest was initiated, he was "conducted by two priests round the altar thrice during . . . singing."[65] One "ancient form of dedication" for a Christian building (dating from the tenth century) dictates that the priests were to go "thrice round the church."[66] A type of clockwise circuit can be detected in the royal accession rites of England when the king turns successively to the four cardinal directions of the church to receive the recognition or approval of the crowd—a group of officiators actually makes the circuit as they question the audience about their acceptance of the new sovereign.[67]

ALMSGIVING

During initiation the Masonic candidate is introduced to the concept of almsgiving, though this "was not one of the original objects for which the institution of Freemasonry was established."[68]

As early as AD 529, a man becoming a Benedictine monk/priest would consecrate his property "to the poor" or donate it to the monastery where he had applied for admission.[69] While the Christian king in England was being put into his office, he offered an ingot of gold at the altar.[70]

INVESTITURE

The Masonic candidate is invested with a white leather apron which is said to be connected with the apparel of the operative stonemasons. Some Masonic scholars understand, however, that in ancient times such an object "was rather an ecclesiastical than a civil decoration," and even around the turn of the twentieth century, its bestowal was "connected with ecclesiastical honors; for the chief dignitaries of the Christian church . . . [were] invested with aprons as a peculiar badge of distinction."[71]

It was common for the ancient Christian catechumens to be invested with a white garment when they were initiated.[72] It is known that the ancient Christian kings were given royal raiment during their accession rites,[73] and the monks had "new garments" or "robes" bestowed upon them also[74]—some of them even receiving leather aprons.[75]

REGALIA

The compass and square are placed on the Masonic altar[76] and are utilized as symbolic instruments[77] to teach moral lessons.[78] Near the end of each of the three initiations, a set of architectural tools is handed to the candidate.[79]

The Christian king's regalia were placed upon the altar of the church where his coronation took place; these included his crown, scepter, rod, swords, orb, and ring.[80] The pieces of regalia were handed to the king at different points in the ritual. Certain items of this regalia were symbolic of moral precepts that were to be exemplified by the king. The scepter, rod, and sword, for example, represented equity, justice, and mercy.[81] The various pieces of clothing the Coptic monks received at their initiations likewise had symbolic precepts attached to them. The symbolism was geared toward "the regulation of the character" of the monk. The clothes signified things such as innocence, the cutting off of worldly deeds and conversation, a good personal work ethic, ministering to others, modesty, subduing one's passions, and always being prepared to preach the gospel.[82] The artworks of medieval Christendom bear witness to the fact that the orthodox Christians not only connected the builder's compass with God as Creator or "Architect of the Universe,"[83] but they also held the builder's square to be a symbol of righteousness.[84] Even in the nonecclesiastical context of 1611 heraldry, a tool of stone-work was assigned symbolic value. The level (line) was seen as a "type of equity and uprightness in all . . . actions."[85]

DEATH AND IMMORTALITY

In the Master Mason's degree, the candidate learns about death and the immortality which follows it. Both of these states are signified in the ritual by symbolic actions.[86] The Graham Manuscript (1726) preserves a strand of Masonic lore wherein the death of Noah and an attempt to raise him was connected with this part of the ceremony.[87]

Christian catechumens experienced a symbolic death, burial, and resurrection on a regular basis: baptism. As noted above, some monks/priests went through a ritualized death (lying prostrate), burial, and a raising when they were initiated. There is evidence for this type of activity at monkish profession in AD 1445.[88] The Christian king is, in some instances, prostrate during the royal rites and then rises after a prayer is said over him.[89] It might also be noted that it was after the king arose from his prostrate position that he was given an article of clothing called an armil.[90] This vestment was representative of the "Divine enfolding"[91] or the embrace of God.[92] Since the example near the beginning of this chapter ties the Kiss of Peace to what happens to the monk after his rising, it should be pointed out that some medieval kings received the Kiss of Peace after lying prostrate during initiation,[93] and medieval bishops and monks were likewise given the Kiss of Peace when they were initiated.[94] St. Augustine mentioned that in his day (AD 354–430), the Kiss of Peace was accompanied by an embrace.[95]

CATECHISM

Each of the three fundamental degrees of Masonic initiation has a catechism associated with it. This catechism is designed to encourage proficiency in the degree that has been received before the Mason advances to the next level.[96]

A catechism is a method of "instruction by word of mouth, especially by questioning and answering." The catechistic method was incorporated into the early Christian initiation experience.[97] A survey of early Christian initiation texts shows that a staple of the initiatory experience was a series of questions and answers exchanged between the catechumen and an officiator.[98] Some of the early Christians were additionally tested as to their knowledge of Christianity; being required to recite a set formula of words (a creed).[99] Monks from the medieval and Reformation eras also had to answer a number of questions from the leader of a monastery when they desired to start the initiation process for a particular religious order.[100] The initiation practices for the Christian kings of England followed the same pattern. An officiator (the archbishop) posed a series of questions which the sovereign was obliged to answer before the assembled crowd.[101] Kings were specifically asked about their religious faith.[102]

NOTES

1. John Hamill, "Whence Come We?" in John Hamill, *Masonic Perspectives* (Australia: Victorian Lodge of Research, 1992), para. 21–23.

2. Fred L. Pick and G. Norman Knight, *The Pocket History of Freemasonry*, 5th ed. (London: Frederick Muller, 1969), 88.

3. Publications of the Regius and Cooke manuscripts can be found in Henry L. Stillson and William J. Hughan, *History of the Ancient and Honorable Fraternity of Free and Accepted Masons and Concordant Orders*, rev. ed. (New York: Fraternity Publishing Company, 1902), 164–85.

4. Franklin Hooper, ed., *The Encyclopaedia Britannica*, 14th ed. (New York: Encyclopaedia Britannica, Inc., 1932), 9:734.

5. Robert L. D. Cooper, *Cracking the Freemasons Code* (New York: Atria Books, 2006), 105.

6. Hamill, "Whence Come We?" para. 9.

7. Albert G. Mackey, *An Encyclopaedia of Freemasonry*, rev. ed. (New York: The Masonic History Company, 1921), 1:449; emphasis in original.

8. Ibid., 2:493; John W. Alkin, *Alkin's Lodge Manual*, 5th ed. (Atlanta: Foote and Davies, 1911), 17.

9. Mackey, *An Encyclopaedia of Freemasonry*, 2:493.

10. See Samuel Lee, *Orbis Miraculum or The Temple of Solomon Portrayed by Scripture Light* (London: John Streater, 1659), foldout between pages 14 and 15.

11. Harry Carr, *The Freemason at Work* (London: Burgess and Son, 1976), 322.

12. See Jane Fawcett, *Historic Floors: Their Care and Conservation* (Oxford: Butterworth-Heinemann, 2001), 19.

13. George M. Martin, comp., *British Masonic Miscellany* (Whitefish, MT: Kessinger Publishing, 2003), 12:20.

14. Mackey, *Encyclopaedia of Freemasonry*, 1:50.

15. See Charles G. Herbermann, ed., *The Catholic*

Encyclopedia (New York: Robert Appleton Company, 1907), 1:350.

16. Ibid.

17. Alex Horne, *Sources of Masonic Symbolism* (Richmond, Virginia: Macoy Publishing, 1981), 68. Some people are of the opinion that specific actions by the Master of a lodge are uniquely Masonic in character but Genesis 37:14; Exodus 19:3–8, and Ezekiel 19:1–11 tend to show that what the Master does has a biblical precedent.

18. *The Catholic Encyclopedia* states that the cathedra or bishop's throne "should have an approach of three steps" (3:439). "Originally, the bishop's cathedra stood in the center of the apse, flanked on either side, though on a lower plane, by the benches of the assisting priests" (ibid., 3:437). A five-step cathedra can be seen in Russell Sturgis, *A Dictionary of Architecture and Building* (New York: Macmillan, 1905), 1:306. Catholic church altars are raised on a platform approached by steps that can range in number from three to five to seven (see Horne, *Sources of Masonic Symbolism,* 68).

19. Modern examples can be found in the Baltimore Basilica, the Belleville, Illinois Cathedral of St. Peter, and the New York City Cathedral of St. Patrick (raised on three steps). A late nineteenth century example can be seen in Chester Cathedral in England.

20. Mackey, *An Encyclopaedia of Freemasonry,* 1:287–88.

21. See Andreas Andreopoulos, *Metamorphosis: The Transfiguration in Byzantine Theology and Iconography* (Crestwood, New York: St. Vladimir's Seminary Press, 2005), 136.

22. 1611 King James Bible. There are several other symbols on this biblical genealogy page that are of interest because the speculative Freemasons incorporated them into their iconographic system. They include the handclasp, the sun, the moon, the stars, the clouds, and skeletal remains representing death.

23. *Ars Quatuor Coronatorum,* vol. 22, 1889, 17.

24. "Unlike most craftsmen, stonemasons were intimately connected to both the religious and secular powers. They worked closely with bishops and priests to build cathedrals, churches and chapels that glorified God, amplified the Holy Mysteries of the Mass and proclaimed the majesty of the Church. . . . Organized guilds [of stonemasons] in the 1300s . . . required [their] members to be faithful Christians" (Mark A. Tabbert, *American Freemasons* [New York: New York University Press, 2005], 19).

25. *Freemasonry Today,* issue 43, Winter 2007/08, 18.

26. Neville B. Cryer, "The Sources of Masonic Practice," Cornerstone Society Lecture, 2004, 1–3. Cryer thinks that this perspective could be "the real Masonic, not the Hiram, Key" (ibid., 3). In another Masonry-centered presentation, Reverend Cryer has pointed out that the catechisms used by the Freemasons of the old Grand Lodge of York were essentially a form of the Christian Mystery Plays (see Neville B. Cryer, "The Grand Lodge of All England at York Ritual: Its Form and Spirit," Cornerstone Society Lecture, 2003, 4). The legend of the Master Mason's degree is an allegory and "all the legends of Freemasonry are more or less allegorical." The Jewish Rabbis employed allegories as teachings devices and so did the early Christians. Because of their allegorical connections to the biblical and spiritual temples, Masonic historians have a special interest in *The Temple of Solomon Portrayed by Scripture Light* by Samuel Lee, and *Solomon's Temple Spiritualized* by John Bunyan (Mackey, *An Encyclopaedia of Freemasonry,* 1:47; see also John M. Neale and Benjamin Webb, trans., *The Symbolism of Churches and Church Ornaments: A Translation of the First Book of the Rationale Divinorum Officiorum Written by William Durandus* [Leeds: T. W. Green, 1843]). The student of Masonic ritual cannot help but notice that its first three degrees are heavily laden with references to, and quotations from, the Bible.

The use of the Old and New Testaments is another important clue about the ultimate origin of Freemasonry's rites.

27. Mackey, *An Encyclopaedia of Freemasonry*, 2:766.

28. Edward C. Whitaker and Maxwell E. Johnson, eds., *Documents of the Baptismal Liturgy*, rev. and exp. (Collegeville, MN: Liturgical Press, 2003), 81, 166, 195, 270, 292; Oswald Burmester, trans., *Ordination Rites of the Coptic Church* (Cairo, Egypt: Society of Coptic Archeology, 1985), 8–9, 79.

29. G. V. Shann, trans., *Book of Needs of the Holy Orthodox Church* (New York: AMS Press, 1969), 4–6, 25, 53, 58, 60.

30. See Mackey, *An Encyclopaedia of Freemasonry*, 2:786.

31. See ibid., 1:43.

32. Alexander Roberts and James Donaldson, eds., *The Ante-Nicene Fathers* (Grand Rapids, MI: Eerdmans, 1956), 7:422.

33. Burmester, trans., *Ordination Rites of the Coptic Church*, 8–9, 15, 79, 81.

34. Whitaker and Johnson, eds., *Documents of the Baptismal Liturgy*, 27, 198–99, 201.

35. See Thomas G. Simons, *Holy People, Holy Place: Rites for the Church's House* (Chicago: Liturgy Training Publications, 1998), 19–20. In one medieval Palm Sunday procession the cross of Christ was used, in a liturgical drama of sorts, to knock on the church door three times (the church representing the Mount of Olives). This signified the reopening of the gates to heaven, which had been closed between the Fall of Adam and the Atonement. "The procession then passed through the 'Golden Gate' to heavenly Jerusalem" (Jan van Herwaarden, *Between Saint James and Erasmus: Studies in Late Medieval Religious Life, Devotion and Pilgrimage in the Netherlands* [Leiden: Brill, 2003], 302). A series of three door knockings (by a bishop) was performed on an antechamber cathedral door at the coronation of a French Christian king in AD 1610 (see János M. Bak, ed., *Coronations: Medieval and Early Modern Monarchic Ritual* [Berkeley: University of California Press, 1990], 44).

36. Mackey, *An Encyclopaedia of Freemasonry,* 1:203; 2:626, 644.

37. Herbermann, ed., *The Catholic Encyclopedia,* 10:469.

38. Burmester, trans., *Ordination Rites of the Coptic Church,* 76, 81–83, 101.

39. See Mackey, *An Encyclopaedia of Freemasonry,* 2:666.

40. Herbermann, ed., *The Catholic Encyclopedia,* 10:348.

41. See Mackey, *An Encyclopaedia of Freemasonry,* 2:578.

42. Ibid.

43. See Bak, ed., *Coronations: Medieval and Early Modern Monarchic Ritual,* 62 fig. 4.1; Anonymous, *A Complete Account of the Ceremonies Observed in the Coronations of the Kings and Queens of England,* 4th ed. (London: Roberts, Stagg, and Browne, 1727), 9.

44. See Shann, trans., *Book of Needs of the Holy Orthodox Church,* 13.

45. See Mackey, *An Encyclopaedia of Freemasonry,* 1:50, 383; 2:577.

46. See Whitaker and Johnson, eds., *Documents of the Baptismal Liturgy,* 45, 48.

47. See Herbermann, ed., *The Catholic Encyclopedia,* 4:381.

48. Reginald M. Woolley, *Coronation Rites* (Cambridge: University Press, 1915), 18–19.

49. Martin Brecht, *Martin Luther: His Road to Reformation, 1483–1521* (Minneapolis, MN: Fortress Press, 1985), 61–62.

50. See Burmester, trans., *Ordination Rites of the Coptic Church,* 9, 11, 82–83, 106.

51. See Mackey, *An Encyclopaedia of Freemasonry,* 1:196–97, 336–37, 446–47.

52. Receiving light is a ubiquitous theme in Whitaker and Johnson, eds., *Documents of the Baptismal Liturgy.*

53. Bak, ed., *Coronations: Medieval and Early Modern Monarchic Ritual,* 157.

54. Mackey, *An Encyclopaedia of Freemasonry,* 2:525.

55. See ibid., 2:524, 624–25.

56. See Whitaker and Johnson, eds., *Documents of the Baptismal Liturgy*, 37, 43–45, 48, 57, 160, 163.

57. Brecht, *Martin Luther: His Road to Reformation, 1483–1521*, 61–62. Monastic vows at an altar are also mentioned in Ethelred L. Taunton, *The English Black Monks of St. Benedict* (New York: Longmans, Green and Co., 1897), 1:75. Some monastic vows were said to be made "in the presence of God and His holy angels . . . [and] in the presence of witnesses" (Oliver J. Thatcher and Edgar H. McNeal, *A Source Book for Mediaeval History* [New York: Charles Scribner's Sons, 1905], 485–86).

58. See Burmester, trans., *Ordination Rites of the Coptic Church*, 9, 11, 82–83, 106; cf. Herbermann, ed., *The Catholic Encyclopedia*, 6:427.

59. Anonymous, *A Complete Account of the Ceremonies Observed in the Coronations of the Kings and Queens of England*, 34. The practice of the Christian king taking a coronation oath "on the Gospels" can be detected in AD 1155 (Woolley, *Coronation Rites*, 46). This was the normal procedure (at the church altar) up to the fifteenth century (see Leopold G. W. Legg, ed., *English Coronation Records* [Westminster: Archibald Canstable and Company, 1901], xxx). During the fealty oath that was enacted at the end of the king's coronation the vassal would place their "hands on the Gospels" (ibid., lvi). "During the Middle Ages oaths were taken by placing both hands on the altar" (Peter Eberle, *Commentary on the Ritual of Monastic Profession for the Swiss American Congregation* [St. Benedict, Oregon: Swiss American Benedictine Congregation, 1984], 24).

60. Mackey, *An Encyclopaedia of Freemasonry*, 2:535, 559.

61. Ibid., 2:522. The secrets of Freemasonry consist of its modes of recognition (see the United Grand Lodge of England website, link path: All about Masonry, What is Freemasonry / Secrecy). Mackey provides important perspectives about these

items. He says, "[A] system of recognition by signs, and words, and grips has existed in the earliest times and, therefore, . . . they were not invented by the Masons who borrowed them, as they did much more of their mystical system, from antiquity" (Mackey, *An Encyclopaedia of Freemasonry,* 2:611). The monks of the Middle Ages utilized a system of signs, and some Masonic historians are of the opinion that the Freemasons "derived their custom of having signs of recognition from the rule of the old monks" (ibid., 2:690). "Some eminent brethren of the [Masonic] fraternity insist that the [Masonic] penalty had its origin in the manner in which the lamb was sacrificed under the charge of the captain of the [Israelite] temple" (ibid., 2:551). Masonic authors admit that some of the Masonic modes of recognition come straight from the Bible (see A. C. F. Jackson, "Masonic Passwords: Their Development and Use in the Early 18th Century," *Ars Quatuor Coronatorum* 87 [1974]: 106–107, 123, 125, 128, 130; Eric Ward, "In the Beginning Was the Word . . ." *Ars Quatuor Coronatorum* 83 [1970]: 309; Colin F. W. Dyer, *Symbolism in Craft Freemasonry* [London: Lewis Masonic, 1983], 49). Indeed, it becomes apparent to the keen observer that a number of the Masonic modes of recognition can be found in the Bible, the ancient artworks of the orthodox Christians, and in orthodox Christian initiation rituals.

62. This is a ubiquitous theme throughout Whitaker and Johnson, eds., *Documents of the Baptismal Liturgy.*

63. Taunton, *The English Black Monks of St. Benedict,* 1:295.

64. See Mackey, *An Encyclopaedia of Freemasonry,* 1:152.

65. Burmester, trans., *Ordination Rites of the Coptic Church,* 11.

66. Neale and Webb, trans., *The Symbolism of Churches and Church Ornaments,* 237. The circumambulation begins at the church door which is later to be entered. Then a deacon enters the church, shuts the door, and stands before it. The bishop (on the other side) strikes the door with his staff and recites part of

the Psalm 24 temple entrance liturgy, "Lift up your heads, O ye gates; and be ye lift[ed] up, ye everlasting doors; and the King of Glory shall come in." The deacon on the other side of the door responds with the question, "Who is the King of Glory?" The bishop and the deacon repeat their dialogue twice more, after which a chorus of people provides the answer, "The Lord of hosts, He is the King of Glory." The bishop then strikes the door again. It is opened and he enters the church. This was the dedication practice of St. Dunstan (ca. AD 909–988) of England (ibid., 237–38).

67. Anonymous, *A Complete Account of the Ceremonies Observed in the Coronations of the Kings and Queens of England,* 28–29.

68. Mackey, *An Encyclopaedia of Freemasonry,* 1:48.

69. Boniface Verheyen, *The Holy Rule of St. Benedict* (Grand Rapids, MI: Christian Classics Ethereal Library, 1949), 14.

70. Legg, ed., *English Coronation Records,* xxvii; Herbermann, ed., *The Catholic Encyclopedia,* 4:384.

71. Mackey, *An Encyclopaedia of Freemasonry,* 1:72.

72. See Whitaker and Johnson, eds., *Documents of the Baptismal Liturgy,* 79, 96, 107, etc.

73. See Herbermann, ed., *The Catholic Encyclopedia,* 4:384.

74. Thatcher and McNeal, *A Source Book for Mediaeval History,* 488. In this medieval source the garments of the monk are "touched with holy oil and sprinkled with water which has been blessed" before they are given to him (ibid.).

75. See *The Metropolitan Museum of Art Bulletin,* vol. 10, no. 7, July 1915, 149–50; Roger S. Bagnall, ed., *Egypt in the Byzantine World 300–700* (New York: Cambridge University Press, 2007), 172. John Cassian (AD 360–433)—a monk and Saint of both the Roman Catholic and Eastern Orthodox churches—listed "the sheepskin or goatskin round the waist and thighs (*melotes, pera, penula*)" which was worn by some of the ancient monks (William Smith and Samuel Cheetham,

A Dictionary of Christian Antiquities [London: John Murray, 1875], 1:753). A "melotes. . . . [seems to be] simply an apron formed of the skin of a beast. . . . a leathern apron" (Galfridus Anglicus and Albert Way, eds., *Promptorium Parvulorum Sive Clericorum: Lexicon Anglo-Latinum Princeps* [London: Camden Society, 1843], 25). Masonic aprons are often decorated with many symbols. The symbols on Masonic aprons should be compared with the symbols found on the aprons of Greek orthodox Christian monks (great schema or angelic habit). For an example of a symbol-decorated gremial or apron owned by a Franciscan archbishop (ca. AD 1528–1537) see Joseph J. Rishel and Suzanne Stratton-Pruitt, *The Arts in Latin America, 1492–1820* (Philadelphia, PA: Philadelphia Museum of Art, 2006), 169. My thanks to Bryce Haymond for bringing this gremiale/apron to my attention.

76. See Mackey, *An Encyclopaedia of Freemasonry,* 1:51.

77. See ibid., 1:173–74, 2:708.

78. See ibid.

79. See ibid., 1:348.

80. See Anonymous, *A Complete Account of the Ceremonies Observed in the Coronations of the Kings and Queens of England,* 30; Bak, ed., *Coronations: Medieval and Early Modern Monarchic Ritual,* 157.

81. Anonymous, *A Complete Account of the Ceremonies Observed in the Coronations of the Kings and Queens of England,* 40.

82. Philip Schaff and Henry Wace, eds., *Nicene and Post-Nicene Fathers,* 2d series (Oxford: Parker and Company, 1894), 11:201–205.

83. Nicola Coldstream, *Medieval Architecture* (New York: Oxford University Press, 2002), 42. The publication in 1619 by John Trundle of a work called *Keepe Within Compasse* demonstrates that in early seventeenth century England non-Masons associated a specific architectural tool with a moral precept

(see Ian M. Green, *Print and Protestantism in Early Modern England* [New York: Oxford University Press, 2000], 405). An "identically structured" publication of about 1630 called *The Mother's Counsell or Live Within Compasse* indicates the prevalence of this idea in English society before the formal institutionalization of speculative Freemasonry (see Alexandra Shepard, *Meanings of Manhood in Early Modern England* [New York: Oxford University Press, 2003], 32). For the illustration on the title page of the men's booklet showing a man standing on a black-and-white checkered floor and an architect's compass above his head see ibid., 31. It should be noted that the title page illustrations of both the men's and women's booklets name the types of characteristics that males and females should keep with compass—gluttony, chastity, etc. (see ibid., 31, 33).

84. See John Lowden, *The Making of the Bibles Moralisées* (University Park, PA: Pennsylvania State University Press, 2000), 1:112–13, 151. For a Bible illustration of Zacharias the temple priest holding a compass to his chest and his wife Elizabeth holding a square to her chest see figure 55 in the same source—at the start of the Gospels. The compass and square also decorate a Roman Catholic church pulpit in Spain which seems to date from between AD 910 and AD 1080 (see *Ars Quatuor Coronatorum,* vol. 32, 1919, 59 and fig. 2). For an illustration dated ca. 1476 that depicts God and angels holding the compass, square, and level respectively (in the context of the creation) see Trenchard Cox, *Jehan Foucquet: Native of Tours* (Freeport, NY: Books for Libraries Press, 1972), facing page 88. Appreciation is extended to Bryce Haymond for bringing this item to my attention. An illustrated Gospel book from England created about AD 1000 reportedly shows the hand of God holding the compass, square, and scales (see *Viator: Medieval and Renaissance Studies,* vol. 2, 1971, 189).

85. John Guillim, *A Display of Herladrie* (London: William Hall, 1611), 208.

86. Mackey, *An Encyclopaedia of Freemasonry,* 1:198, 2:474–75.

87. A photographic reproduction of the entire Graham Manuscript can be seen in *Ars Quatuor Coronatorum,* vol. 50, 1937, between pages 16 and 17.

88. See Eberle, *Commentary on the Ritual of Monastic Profession for the Swiss American Congregation,* 35–39.

89. Legg, ed., *English Coronation Records,* xxviii–xxix.

90. See ibid., xxviii–xxix, xlii.

91. Herbermann, ed., *The Catholic Encyclopedia,* 12:714.

92. See Anonymous, *A Complete Account of the Ceremonies Observed in the Coronations of the Kings and Queens of England,* 38.

93. See Bak, ed., *Coronations: Medieval and Early Modern Monarchic Ritual,* 55, 64, 159.

94. See Burmester, trans., *Ordination Rites of the Coptic Church,* 114–15; Taunton, *The English Black Monks of St. Benedict,* 1:75; Brecht, *Martin Luther: His Road to Reformation, 1483–1521,* 61–62.

95. "The 'Peace be with you' is said, and the Christians embrace one another with the holy kiss" (Mary S. Muldowney, trans., *Saint Augustine: Sermons on the Liturgical Seasons* [New York: Fathers of the Church, Inc., 1959], 197).

96. Mackey, *An Encyclopaedia of Freemasonry,* 1:136–37.

97. See Everett Ferguson, ed., *Encyclopedia of Early Christianity,* 2d ed. (New York: Garland Publishing, 1999), 1:223–24.

98. Whitaker and Johnson, eds., *Documents of the Baptismal Liturgy,* 33, 42, etc. Questions and answers would occasionally be exchanged at the front door of the church (ibid., 74–76, 187, 199). These exchanges are sometimes referred to as scrutinies (see Herbermann, ed., *The Catholic Encyclopedia,* 13:641).

99. Whitaker and Johnson, eds., *Documents of the Baptismal Liturgy,* 34.

100. See Thatcher and McNeal, *A Source Book for Mediaeval History*, 489–90; Taunton, *The English Black Monks of St. Benedict*, 1:293–94; Brecht, *Martin Luther: His Road to Reformation, 1483–1521*, 58–59.

101. See Anonymous, *A Complete Account of the Ceremonies Observed in the Coronations of the Kings and Queens of England*, 33–34.

102. See Woolley, *Coronation Rites*, 49.

CHAPTER 4

Freemasonry in Nauvoo

When the Latter-day Saints occupied Nauvoo, Illinois, in the year 1842, there were approximately four thousand residents inside the city limits (twelve thousand by 1844),[1] but only thirty Mormons in the general area had membership in the Masonic fraternity. Among this small group were such notable men as Hyrum Smith (the Prophet's brother), Heber C. Kimball (an Apostle), John Smith (the Prophet's uncle), Newel K. Whitney (a bishop), and George Miller (another bishop).[2]

A resident of Nauvoo by the name of Ebenezer Robinson recalled that the leaders of the LDS Church "strenuously opposed secret societies" until the conversion to Mormonism of John C. Bennett—who had previously been initiated as a Freemason—and then "a great change in sentiment seemed to take place."[3] Bennett had been called upon to assume Sidney Rigdon's role as counselor in the First Presidency of the Church "until" the latter had recovered from an ailment.[4] It appears that the choice of Bennett as Rigdon's replacement was influenced partly by the fact that they knew each other prior to Brother Rigdon's conversion to Mormonism[5] and also because on the day before Bennett's formal assignment as a temporary stand-in, Rigdon had requested him "to officiate in his place."[6]

THE PETITION FOR A LODGE

The available evidence suggests that it was shortly before 28 June 1841 that John Bennett spearheaded a petition to Bodley Lodge No. 1 in Quincy, Illinois, to recommend to the state's Grand Lodge that the Masonic organization be formally established in Nauvoo.[7] This petition was denied because the members of Bodley Lodge were not familiar with any of the Mormon

Masons. Thus, they could not properly exercise their judgment with regard to the request that had been made.

After this refusal had taken place, another petition was sent to Columbus Lodge No. 6—supposedly at the instigation of George Miller, John D. Parker, and Lucius N. Scovil. The "Master, Wardens, and Brethren" of that lodge vouched to Grand Master Abraham Jonas of the Grand Lodge of Illinois that the petitioners were "worthy and fit" Freemasons. Upon this favorable recommendation, Grand Master Jonas issued, on 15 October 1841, a dispensation for the formation of the Nauvoo Lodge with the three aforementioned Mormons acting as its main officers.

In evaluating this incident, it should be considered that perhaps the recommendation of Columbus Lodge was not the only thing that influenced Grand Master Jonas's decision. The Deputy Grand Master of the Grand Lodge of Illinois from 1840 to 1843 was none other than James Adams, a probate judge living in Springfield, who seems to have been on the verge of conversion into The Church of Jesus Christ of Latter-day Saints by 24 October 1839.[8] Adams became personally acquainted with Joseph Smith on 4 November 1839 and treated the Prophet as if he were a member of his own family.[9] It therefore seems likely that the Deputy Grand Master would have exerted a degree of positive influence on behalf of his religious colleagues.

There is no evidence that Joseph Smith played a direct role in trying to get a Masonic lodge established among the Saints, though it must be admitted that the Masons adhered to principles that would have been especially attractive to the leader of a frequently (and recently) persecuted people. "Freemasonry is one of the strongest binding contracts that exists between man and man," said Elder John Taylor of the Quorum of the Twelve Apostles.[10] And according to Apostle and Master Mason Heber C. Kimball, a member of that society could expect other Masons to step forward in time of need to render assistance. These fraternal brothers were expected to be faithful to each other "in every case and under every circumstance, the commission of crime excepted."[11]

Even if it cannot be demonstrated that the Prophet instigated the process of bringing the Masonic organization to Nauvoo, it appears that he chose to join himself with them for a very specific purpose. Lorenzo Snow, who was serving a mission in England at the time when Masonry was being established in Nauvoo, expressed his understanding late in the nineteenth century that the Prophet and other Illinois Church members joined Freemasonry in order to "obtain influence in furtherance of the purposes of the Lord."[12]

By the very end of December 1841, a small group of Nauvoo Freemasons met in Hyrum Smith's business office to accept Grand Master Jonas's dispensation and to begin the process of forming their lodge's administrative and governmental structures. On December 30th, the Prophet Joseph Smith and forty-one other men "preferred petitions for membership" in the Masonic organization and at some point paid a five dollar fee for the privilege of receiving the first degree (additional costs were three dollars for the second degree and seven dollars for the third). A committee of investigation was formed to scrutinize the lives of the applicants, and on 3 February 1842, they reported favorably on the Prophet's request for admittance into their ranks. He was then "balloted for [by the Masons who were present] and the ballot [was] found clear."[13]

Formal preparations for the installation of the new lodge were considered by the existing Masons of Nauvoo on 17 February 1842, and it was recorded in the lodge's minute book under that date that the LDS First Presidency and Quorum of the Twelve Apostles would be invited to participate in the procession and public exercises of the day. It was further noted that Grand Master Abraham Jonas of the Grand Lodge of Illinois would play a role in these important events. Jonas, who was born to Jewish parents in Exeter, England, had been elected to his high Masonic office on 28 April 1840.[14]

INSTALLATION DAY

The public installation ceremonies for the Nauvoo Lodge took place on 15 March 1842 at one in the afternoon after a procession was formed and made its way to the grove of trees near the west side of the temple. The historical records regarding the installation are sparse, but they do provide a few valuable insights. First, they relate that the Prophet was invited to officiate on this occasion in the capacity of "Grand Chaplain," even though he was not yet a Freemason. In Albert G. Mackey's encyclopedia of Freemasonry it is said that the office of Grand Chaplain was connected with the Grand Lodge, not a local lodge, and the duties of the person who served in that capacity were "confined to offering up prayer at the communications of the Grand Lodge, and conducting its devotional exercises on public occasions."[15] In other words, Joseph Smith's stint as Grand Chaplain was honorary and only lasted for a short period of time.[16] The records of the Nauvoo Lodge do not indicate that the Prophet ever served as a chaplain for that local organization.

A second insight is that "universal satisfaction was manifested" with regard to the installation proceedings.[17] In a letter to the editor of the *Columbus Advocate* dated 22 March 1842 (and reprinted in the *Times and Seasons*), an anonymous visitor to Nauvoo who some people think was Jonas himself reported that an immense crowd attended the public installation of the lodge's officers, yet this unidentified observer commented that this gathering of Saints was the most behaved and best-dressed assembly they had ever seen; there were no drunken or disorderly persons anywhere to be found.[18]

A third insight, which is furnished by the Nauvoo Lodge records, is that Grand Master Jonas delivered a polished address on Ancient York Masonry to the crowd gathered before him.[19] It is not known exactly what the Grand Master told the citizens of Nauvoo about the organization he was establishing that day in their midst. But since the designation of Ancient York Masonry tied this society directly to England, it is natural to suppose that the lecture contained material which had been gleaned from the Old Charges of English Masonry. In which case, the Saints were probably told the legendary tale of Freemasonry stretching back in time to the builders of King Solomon's Temple. If this point was, in fact, brought up during the lecture, it would surely have piqued the interest of the Latter-day Saints since the revelation now known as Doctrine and Covenants section 124 had been received on 19 January 1841 and was openly published in Nauvoo by June of that same year.[20] In this revelation, the Lord spoke of restoring ordinances through Joseph Smith that had once been practiced by the Israelites in a "house buil[t] in the land of promise," meaning King Solomon's Temple (D&C 124:38).

INITIATED, PASSED, AND RAISED

Joseph Smith's actual initiation as a Freemason took place over a two-day period. The Prophet received the first degree of Entered Apprentice on 15 March 1842 at 7:00 PM in the upper room of his redbrick store. Heber C. Kimball recorded that Abraham Jonas himself "acted as Master" of the lodge during these particular proceedings.[21] Before these rituals took place, however, Grand Master Jonas had a special dispensation read out loud to the assembled Freemasons. In this document, he declared that Joseph Smith's petition for admission to Masonry could be received and acted upon without delay, so long as he went through the balloting process once again and it was found to be unanimously clear. In this case, said the document, the Prophet could then receive the three degrees of Ancient York Masonry "as speedily as the nature of the case [would] admit"—so long as the ancient landmarks of the order and the lodge's own bylaws were strictly adhered to. With the balloting process completed again, and found to be free of objection, the Prophet was "duly initiated" as an Entered Apprentice Mason.[22]

At 9:00 AM on 16 March 1842, the Prophet Joseph Smith met once more with the Nauvoo Lodge in the second story of his mercantile establishment and indicated his desire "to be advanced in Masonry." Once his proficiency in the previous degree had been vouched for, another ballot was held and cleared, and President Smith "duly received and passed to the degree of F[ellow] C[raft]." At 2:00 PM on the same day, the Prophet applied to be inducted into the Master Mason degree, and after the ballot was taken and passed, he was "duly raised to said degree" and signed the bylaws of the lodge.[23] It is of interest to note that during all three of the Prophet's initiations, his brother Hyrum Smith was acting as the Senior Warden of the lodge.

It is often said by commentators on the subject of Mormonism and Masonry that Joseph Smith became a Mason "at sight." If it is meant by this phrase that he was allowed to go through all three of the initiation degrees—in physical sight of the Grand Master—without submitting to the typical waiting period between them, then such is a correct characterization. However, it would not be correct to say that the Prophet became a Freemason without experiencing the full initiation rites, but simply had the status bestowed upon him by verbal decree of the Grand Master. The records of the Nauvoo Lodge have time stamps attached to all of the initiation notices, and they also contain a set of consistent key phrases. If Joseph Smith's time stamps and phrases are compared with the regular workings of the lodge after the installation took place, then it can be seen that his initiation time frames and phrases match those of all the other Masons. The fact that it took two days to completely induct the Prophet into Masonry's degrees argues strongly against the "decree theory" or even the proposition that the

Church President might have been made a Mason by receiving an extremely abbreviated set of rites. It is self-evident that he was not required to memorize each Masonic ritual before advancing to the next stage of initiation but it is also recorded in the lodge minutes that his proficiency was vouched for in one degree before he continued on to the next.

EVALUATING THE DATA

In appraising the Prophet's connection to Freemasonry, it is important to understand the amount of affiliation that he had with it. Below is a chart that illustrates the days when the Nauvoo Lodge convened for business and Joseph Smith's schedule for attending lodge meetings[24] before he first administered the temple endowment ceremony to a small group of Latter-day Saints on 4 May 1842. The capitalized initials within this chart represent the various initiation ceremonies that Joseph Smith witnessed in the Nauvoo Lodge on the days indicated. E.A. = Entered Apprentice; F.C. = Fellow Craft; M.M. = Master Mason.

DATE	DEGREE
15 March 1842	E.A.
16 March 1842	F.C. M.M. (twice)
17 March 1842	
7 April 1842	E.A.
8 April 1842	
9 April 1842	E.A.
11 April 1842	
12 April 1842	
13 April 1842	E.A. F.C. M.M.
14 April 1842	E.A. F.C. M.M.

15 April 1842

16 April 1842

18 April 1842

19 April 1842

20 April 1842

21 April 1842

22 April 1842

23 April 1842

25 April 1842

26 April 1842

27 April 1842

28 April 1842

29 April 1842

30 April 1842

2 May 1842

3 May 1842

The above chart indicates that before Joseph Smith introduced the full temple ceremonies among the Nauvoo Saints (on
4 May 1842), he witnessed the Masonic initiation rites of an
Entered Apprentice five times, a Fellow Craft three times, and
a Master Mason four times. Then there was a nineteen-day gap
wherein he did not attend any Masonic meetings.

When the Prophet's attendance record at the Nauvoo Lodge
is weighed against the number of times that it actually met
between his formal induction and the bestowal of the Nauvoo
Temple ordinances, it appears that his attachment to Masonry
may not have been as great as some commentators have believed.
The lodge convened on twenty-four separate days during this
time period (sometimes meeting several times per day), but

President Smith only attended on four of those days—or roughly 16.5 percent of the time. And he only witnessed a full set of Masonic ceremonies on two of the four days of his attendance.

On each of the four days when the Prophet was present in the lodge, it should be noted that either members of his immediate family, members of the Quorum of the Twelve Apostles, or members of the Nauvoo Temple building committee were involved in the initiatic proceedings of the day. Therefore, the Prophet's presence in the lodge on those occasions may have simply been an indication of support for his siblings, his closest ecclesiastical associates, and the people who were in charge of raising the Lord's temple.[25] As a full-fledged member of the lodge Joseph Smith would have been involved in casting positive ballots for these individuals on each of these occasions. The days of attendance and the related circumstances were as follows:

- 7 April 1842 (initiation of Brigham Young and Willard Richards)

- 9 April 1842 (initiation of Samuel Smith, William Smith, Brigham Young, and Willard Richards)

- 13 April 1842 (initiation of Samuel Smith and William Smith)

- 14 April 1842 (Hyrum Smith acting as the Master of the lodge; initiation of Elias Higbee and Reynolds Cahoon—members of the Nauvoo Temple building committee[26])

THE FORTY-EIGHT-DAY INTERIM

There were forty-eight days between the day when Joseph Smith became a Master Mason (16 March 1842) and the day when he gave the Nauvoo-era temple endowment to nine men in the upper room of his redbrick store (4 May 1842). Below is an abbreviated day-by-day accounting of what the Prophet is known to have been doing during this time frame.[27] This information helps to put the emergence of the temple rituals into proper historical perspective.

17 March—organized the Relief Society

18 March—at home and the office, engaged in temporal and spiritual business

19 March—at home and the office, engaged in temporal and spiritual business

20 March—preached to a large assembly near the temple

21 March—attended to a financial settlement for money and property

22 March—at the general business office all day

23 March—in council at the office

24 March—attended a meeting of the Relief Society

25 March—attended to business and counseling

26 March—gave instruction for a foreign missionary

27 March—spoke on baptism for the dead; baptized 107 people

28 March—a variety of business at the office

29 March—a variety of business at the office

30 March—a variety of business at the office; instructed the Relief Society on their connection to "the ancient Priesthood" and becoming "a kingdom of priests"

31 March—in council with the elders at the office

1 April—engaged at the general business office; published a lengthy article on trying the spirits; edited and published a portion of the serialized Church history

2 April—one business transaction

3 April—unknown activity

4 April—two business transactions

5 April—one business transaction

6 April—LDS Church conference

7 April—LDS Church conference; spoke about the Nauvoo Temple

8 April—LDS Church conference

9 April—spoke at a funeral; attended the city council meeting

10 April—preached a sermon

11 April—attended the Masonic lodge (this is not attested to in the lodge minutes, but it is known that Hyrum Smith was present in the lodge this day)

12 April—attended the Masonic lodge (this is not attested to in the lodge minutes, but it is known that Hyrum Smith, Samuel Smith, and William Smith were all present in the lodge this day); Apostles spoke about the Nauvoo Temple in the lodge room

13 April—introduced six men into the lodge room (the Nauvoo Lodge minutes verify that the Prophet was present on this day, but the type of "introduction" that he gave is unclear. There were, however, six men other than Joseph Smith who were listed in the lodge minutes as "members")

14 April—met with a lawyer about bankruptcy

15 April—published an article on baptism for the dead; edited and published a portion of the serialized Church history

16 April—unknown activity

17 April—spent the day with family

18 April—testified in court at Carthage, Illinois, regarding bankruptcy

19 April—examined land in the north part of Nauvoo

20 April—assisted in surveying land

21 April—unknown activity

22 April—at the office, conducting temporal and spiritual business

23 April—at the office, conducting temporal and spiritual business

24 April—preached about building the Nauvoo Temple

25 April—mostly with family; reading, meditation, etc.

26 April—mostly with family; reading, meditation, etc.

27 April—mostly with family; reading, meditation, etc.

28 April—attended to Nauvoo Legion business; lectured to the Relief Society and said the Church would be organized in its proper order once the Nauvoo Temple was completed; spoke of delivering "the keys of the Priesthood" to the Church and women receiving them in connection with their husbands; these keys would enable them to "know how to ask the Lord and receive an answer"; said the "keys of the kingdom" were about to be given to others so that they might "be able to detect everything false"; taught themes of the devil having power to deceive, rending the veil and coming into the presence of God, and the building up of Zion

29 April—dealt with a conspiracy against the peace of the Smith household

30 April—signed deeds, spent most of the day with family and James Adams (who would participate in the first endowment on May 4th)

1 May—preached on the "keys of the kingdom," which included "certain signs and words" to be revealed in the Nauvoo Temple by which false spirits could be detected; by these keys one would be "endowed with power"; mentioned the holy of holies of the temple

2 May—published an editorial on "The Temple"; edited and published a portion of the serialized Church history

3 May—mostly with family; with others arranging the upper room of redbrick store like a temple in order to prepare for the bestowal of the endowment

Three things should be noticed about the above timeline. First, when it comes to things Masonic, the *History of the Church* does not always comport with what is recorded in the minutes of the Nauvoo Lodge, which may possibly be explained by the fact that this portion of the history was not composed until after the Prophet's death, and the historian may have been relying upon sketchy notes or imprecise memories. Second, Joseph Smith was an exceptionally busy man who had little time to prepare for the inauguration of the endowment, but it is clear from his activities during this time frame that the temple and its ordinances were never far from his mind. Third, there was a three-day period between the 25th and the 27th of April where Joseph Smith had time to read and reflect. Even though the subject of his study and meditation is unknown, it seems more than a coincidence that the day before and the day after this short period, the Prophet was focused on the temple and its ideology. The implication is that these three days were the time during which the endowment was formalized to the point that it could be presented to the inaugural group of Latter-day Saints on May 4th.

NOTES

1. See *Brigham Young University Studies*, vol. 35, no. 2, 1995, 93; hereafter cited as *BYUS*.

2. See Mervin B. Hogan, *The Founding Minutes of Nauvoo Lodge* (Des Moines, IA: Research Lodge Number 2, 1971), 3–4, 9–11. Heber C. Kimball inexplicably noted in an account written three years after the fact that on the day the Nauvoo Lodge was installed (15 March 1842) there were "forty members" (*BYUS*, vol. 15, no. 4, Summer 1975, 458–59).

3. *The Return*, vol. 2, no. 6, June 1890, 287.

4. Brigham H. Roberts, ed., *History of the Church* (Salt Lake City: Deseret News Press, 1930), 4:341; hereafter cited as *HC*.

5. See Andrew C. Skinner, "John C. Bennett: For Prophet or Profit?" in H. Dean Garrett, ed., *Regional Studies in Latter-day Saint Church History: Illinois* (Provo, UT: BYU Department of Church History and Doctrine, 1995), 250.

6. *HC*, 4:339.

7. Bennett appears to be the primary petitioner as per the Quincy, Illinois, Bodley Lodge No. 1 minutes for 28 June 1841 (see Joseph E. Morcombe, *History of Grand Lodge of Iowa* [Cedar Rapids, IA: Grand Lodge of Iowa, 1910], 1:145–46).

8. See Glen M. Leonard, *Nauvoo: A Place of Peace, A People of Promise* (Salt Lake City and Provo, UT: Deseret Book and BYU Press, 2002), 711 n. 34.

9. See *HC*, 4:20.

10. George D. Watt, ed., *Journal of Discourses* (Liverpool, England: Franklin D. and Samuel W. Richards, 1854–1886), 10:125.

11. *Woman's Exponent*, vol. 9, no. 20, 15 March 1881, 154.

12. Stan Larsen, ed., *A Ministry of Meetings: The Apostolic Diaries of Rudger Clawson* (Salt Lake City: Signature Books and Smith Research Associates, 1993), 316. There may be a hint of this idea in the writings of Heber C. Kimball just one month after the Nauvoo Lodge was established. After speaking

about the lodge's founding, he said, "I think it will result in good" (*BYUS*, vol. 15, no. 4, Summer 1975, 458). A statement made by President Brigham Young in 1860 also lends support to the notion that the Saints had hoped their attachment to Freemasonry would engender a social support system. He said with specific reference to the Masons, "The truth is that we have got to look to the Lord God of Israel to sustain us and not to any institution or kingdom or people upon the earth" (Scott G. Kenney, ed., *Wilford Woodruff's Journal* [Midvale, UT: Signature Books, 1985], 5:483).

13. Hogan, *The Founding Minutes of Nauvoo Lodge*, 4, 6, 8, 10.

14. See Isaac Markens, *Abraham Lincoln and the Jews* (New York: Isaac Markens, 1909), 17.

15. *HC*, 4:550; Albert G. Mackey, *An Encyclopaedia of Freemasonry*, rev. ed. (New York: The Masonic History Company, 1921), 1:142.

16. The "office of Chaplain of a Lodge is one which is not recognized in the ritual" of the United States of America, though it is "often conferred by courtesy. The Master of a Lodge in general performs the duties of a Chaplain" (ibid.).

17. *HC*, 4:551.

18. See *Times and Seasons*, vol. 3, no. 11, 1 April 1842, 749–50; hereafter cited as *T&S*.

19. See Hogan, *The Founding Minutes of Nauvoo Lodge*, 12.

20. See *T&S*, vol. 2, no. 15, 1 June 1841, 424–29.

21. *BYUS*, vol. 15, no. 4, Summer 1975, 459.

22. Hogan, *The Founding Minutes of Nauvoo Lodge*, 12.

23. Ibid., 13.

24. See ibid., 11–29 for the days when the lodge met between the Prophet's own Masonic initiation and the day he administered the Nauvoo-era endowment.

25. See ibid., 14–16, 17–18.

26. See *T&S*, vol. 1, no. 12, October 1840, 186.

27. This material is drawn from volume 4 of the *History of the Church*.

CHAPTER 5

Return to Mount Zion

The theory that Joseph Smith took ritual elements from the Freemasons in order to create the LDS temple ceremony is principally founded upon the concept of time. Supporters of this theory argue that since the Prophet joined the Masonic fraternity shortly before he introduced the Nauvoo endowment among the Saints—and because there are similarities between the two sets of ceremonies—the leader of the Mormons must have been guilty of unacknowledged borrowing from the Masons.

On the surface this theory seems to be well-reasoned and based on sound logic. The impression it gives to the casual observer is that they are looking at a solidly built structure. But when a much broader survey of time is taken by the student of the past and the events of history are scrutinized in a much more careful manner, then this theory takes on the appearance of a movie façade; it is not nearly as sturdy as it looks.

The chronologically arranged information in this chapter is centered on the life and teachings of Joseph Smith from the time of the angel Moroni visits in 1823 up until shortly before he was inducted into Freemasonry's rites. It is designed to give the reader a substantial sense of how much the Prophet knew about the Nauvoo-era temple ordinances before March 1842 and when he knew it. This listing is by no means meant to be exhaustive. There is a great deal more that could be said. But because of the sacred nature of temple activity, many references to ritual matters and language have been left out of this listing. Despite this limitation, it should become obvious to the reader that there are many things not explained by the imagination of the theorists.

THE TESTIMONY OF TIME

In 1823 Joseph Smith received a visitation from an angel of God, and that heavenly messenger taught the Prophet many temple-related concepts, all of which were directly connected with the "work" that the Lord had for him to do. The Prophet learned from this angel about the Lord coming to His "temple," about "the covenant," "the sons of Levi" or temple priests and an "offering" that they would make in the Lord's sanctuary (Mal. 3:1–4). Joseph also became aware that the prophet Elijah was somehow going to "reveal . . . the Priesthood" and that there would be a latter-day focus on "the promises made to the fathers" (Mal. 4:5–6). He further learned about praying on "mount Zion" (Joel 2:32),[1] receiving the Lord's "law" or "ways" inside the temple (Isa. 2:2–3), and obtaining blessings associated with adoption, heirship, and immunity from the destroying angel. The Prophet was also shown a vision of these things while they were being told to him,[2] but they were not fully implemented among the Latter-day Saints until the Nauvoo Temple period.

On 15 May 1829, Joseph Smith received "the priesthood of Aaron" or ancient temple priesthood of the Levites (see Ex. 40:12–15;[3] Num. 8:9–11, 13–15) from the resurrected John the Baptist,[4] who was himself a temple priest (see Luke 1:5, 13). The historical record reports, "We received under his hand the holy priesthood, [and] he said, 'upon you my fellow servants, in the name of Messiah I confer this priesthood and this authority, which shall remain upon earth, that the sons of Levi may yet offer an offering unto the Lord in righteousness!'"[5] Thus would be fulfilled the prophecy uttered by the angel who visited Joseph Smith in 1823 (cf. Mal. 3:3). The priesthood of Melchizedek was also vouchsafed to the Prophet in 1829;[6] a priesthood that was conferred upon the kings of ancient Israel when they were initiated in the temple precincts on Mount Zion (see Ps. 2:6, 110:4).

In the years 1829 and 1830, Joseph Smith produced two scriptural texts containing numerous ritual elements that would become familiar to recipients of the Nauvoo endowment. Chapters 2–6 in the book of Mosiah, chapters 11–18 in the book of 3 Nephi, and chapters 2 and 3 in the book of Ether should all be compared with each other in order to see the relevant repeating pattern in the Book of Mormon. Then this same pattern should be sought for in chapter 1 of the book of Moses while chapters 2–6 of the same volume can be examined for other patterns that were employed in Nauvoo. In 1834 some portions of the book of Moses that were later incorporated into the Nauvoo-era temple liturgy were interwoven into Lecture on Faith #2 (cf. D&C 29:34–45).

Sometime in September 1830, Parley P. Pratt (who would later be ordained as an Apostle) was traveling on foot after preaching the gospel to a group of non-Mormons. "The sky was without a cloud," he said; "the stars shone out beautifully, and all nature seemed reposing in quiet." While meditating upon the content of the scriptures as he walked, his "attention was aroused by a sudden appearance of a brilliant light which shone around [him], above the brightness of the sun." On looking upward, he saw a long chain of red light which proceeded—over the course of several minutes—to form itself, through "exact movements," into three distinct geometrical shapes before fading away. Parley attributed the origin of this vision to the Lord and identified the symbols that he saw as those "known only to the wise."[7]

Joseph Smith was shown a vision on 16 February 1832 wherein he learned about three increasingly more glorious kingdoms or degrees of existence (see D&C 76). He also became aware that the highest or celestial degree, where the "presence of God" was found (v. 62), was connected with "Mount Zion" (the temple mountain in the Old Testament) and the "city of . . . God," which is "the holiest of all" (v. 66)—a clear reference to the cubic city or heavenly Holy of Holies in the New Testament.

Furthermore, Joseph was informed that persons who resided there would be "sealed by the Holy Spirit of promise" (v. 53) and attain to membership in the Church of the Firstborn (see vv. 54, 67, 71, 94, 102); they would be "kings" and "priests of the Most High, after the order of Melchizedek" (vv. 56–57); they would receive the Father's "fulness" (vv. 56, 71, 94), meaning that they would inherit "all things" (vv. 55, 59) including the "glory" of the Father (v. 56), who would make them "equal in power, and in might, and in dominion." In other words, they would become "gods" (v. 58). In addition, the Prophet was taught during this visionary experience about the origin and nature of Lucifer and his followers (see vv. 25–38, 44), and also about "the mysteries of [God's] kingdom" which "are not lawful for man to utter" (vv. 114–15). One notation in the D&C 76 revelation should not be overlooked. In verse 60 it is said that the kings and priests of the celestial realm "shall overcome all things." On 12 November 1835, the Prophet Joseph Smith taught that the "endowment" associated with the temple was necessary so that individuals would be "prepared and able to overcome all things."[8]

Section 84 of the Doctrine and Covenants was given to Joseph Smith on the 22nd and 23rd of September 1832. In this revelation, the Lord instructed the Saints that they were to establish a modern-day "Mount Zion" (vv. 2, 32) and build a temple therein (see vv. 3–4). The Saints were to become "sons of Moses and Aaron" (see vv. 6, 18, 30–32, 34) and, like their ancient temple counterparts, they were to "offer an acceptable offering and sacrifice in the house of the Lord" (v. 31). Since the Lord specified in the Book of Mormon that after the Atonement of Jesus Christ had been wrought, He would not "accept" any more blood "sacrifices and . . . offerings" (3 Ne. 9:19), the question naturally arises about what type of "acceptable" sacrifices and offerings the Saints were going to perform in the new "Mount Zion" sanctuary. This question was answered in 1841, when the Lord gave instructions about the ordinances that would take place inside the Nauvoo Temple (see D&C 124:39). Since the Old Testament temple priests were required to wear special clothing when they made sacrifices and offerings at the altar (see Ex. 28:2, 40–43), the idea of latter-day liturgical vestments would have become relevant when D&C 84 was delivered. Yet such ceremonial items were not implemented among the Saints until the Nauvoo period. D&C 84 also presented the Prophet with themes such as "the mysteries of the kingdom" (v. 19), "oath and covenant" (v. 39–41), becoming sanctified (see v. 23), entering into God's presence through Melchizedek priesthood ordinances (see vv. 19–22), inheriting all that God has (see v. 38), and receiving the "fulness" of His glory (v. 24).

On 1 June 1833, the Lord indicated through revelation that He would show the pattern for constructing the Kirtland Temple to three individuals (see D&C 95:13–14). This would be a house of endowment, instruction, and prayer as well as a site where the Saints could make an "offering" (vv. 8, 16–17). Temple architect Truman O. Angell recalled that sometime in the fall of 1835, "Joseph [Smith] came into the [lower] hall [of the Kirtland Temple]. The leading mechanic, John Carl, by profession a carriage builder, wanted to seat the house contrary to what Joseph had proposed. Joseph answered him that he had seen the inside of every building that had been built unto the Lord upon this earth and he hated to have to say so."[9]

During 1833 Joseph Smith was working on a revision of the texts of the Bible. In relation to the Mount Sinai experience (which has a definite temple backdrop), he wrote, "And the Lord said unto Moses, 'Hew thee two other tables of stone, like unto the first, and I will write upon them also, the words of the law, according as they were written at the first on the tables which thou brakest; but it shall not be according to the first, for I will take away the priesthood out of [the Israelite's] midst; therefore my holy order, and the ordinances thereof, shall not go before them; for my presence shall not go up in their midst, lest I destroy them. But I will give unto them the law as at the first, but it shall be after the law of a carnal commandment; for I have sworn in my wrath, that they shall not enter into my presence, into my rest, in the days of their pilgrimage. Therefore do as I have commanded thee, and be ready in the morning, and come up in the morning unto mount Sinai, and present thyself there to me, in the top of the mount'" (JST, Ex. 34:1–2; cf. D&C 88:34, 36, 121, 123–125). The ideas of coming into the Lord's presence (at the figurative top of the mountain) through the priesthood-based ordinances of the holy order not only echo the teachings of D&C 84, but they also formed the basis of the rituals of the temple in Nauvoo, Illinois.

Near the close of 1833, Elizabeth Tyler had "a remarkable vision." The walls of her house became transparent, and in the open space above her, "she saw a man sitting upon a white cloud, clothed in white from head to foot. He had on a peculiar cap, different from any she had ever seen, with a white robe, underclothing, and moccasins. It was revealed to her that this person was Michael, the Archangel." Shortly thereafter, the Prophet Joseph Smith arrived at her home, and she informed him about what she had seen. "The Prophet informed her that she had had a true vision, and it was of the Lord. He had seen the same angel several times."[10]

In March 1834, the First Presidency of the LDS Church, in continuing a lengthy epistle to congregations scattered abroad, noted that those Saints who become members of the Church of the Firstborn are to receive white linen clothing and a crown, be made kings and priests, be seated upon the Lord's throne to reign, and also be admitted into the heavenly marriage feast.[11]

At the end of 1834, Joseph Smith participated in the preparation of the Lectures on Faith, and they were subsequently presented to some of the elders of the LDS Church. Several of the themes taught by these theological treatises included the creation, the Garden of Eden, the serpent, the Fall, a veil separating God and man but through which the Lord's voice could still be heard, angelic instruction on redemption, ritual practices, obtaining knowledge of God through service and prayer, returning to God's presence, receiving God's fullness (becoming like Him in glory), becoming heirs, and obtaining eternal life (sacrifice being necessary thereto). Most of these lectures were followed by a series of catechetical questions and answers.[12] One participant in the 1835–36 "theological school"—which was superintended by Joseph Smith—said that he received "much good instructions preparatory to the endowment."[13]

The year 1835 saw the introduction of the concept of eternal marriage among the Latter-day Saints in two forms. In a letter written by William W. Phelps and published in the Church's newspaper, he stated that mortality was a time to prepare oneself for a kingdom of glory and that those who became "archangels [or] the sons of God" in the next life would receive "a consummation of glory, and happiness, and perfection," which would include having a spouse "in the Lord."[14] When the first hymnal of the Church was published, it included a song on marriage that spoke of Adam and Eve being united by the Lord in the Garden of Eden. It ended with the note that "union is eternal" in the "perfection" of Zion where Jesus Christ reigns.[15]

On 16 January 1836, the brethren were washed with water so that they might attain a state of "purification" before the Lord. They then covenanted "to be faithful to God." As they performed the washing ceremony, they reflected upon "how the priests anciently used to wash always before ministering before the Lord."[16] On the 21st day of the same month, the brethren received an "anointing with . . . holy oil," and they were "anointed with the same kind of oil and in the [same manner as] were Moses and Aaron and those who stood before the Lord in ancient days." After this ordinance was performed, "the heavens were opened to many,"[17] including the Prophet Joseph Smith. He saw a vision of the gate leading into the celestial kingdom and the manner whereby the Quorum of the Twelve Apostles were admitted through that portal and led into the presence of God.[18] Joseph also learned during this vision that certain types of people who died without receiving authoritative baptism during mortality could end up inheriting the celestial kingdom (see D&C 138), but he was not shown that proxy baptism would be the means of accomplishment. Brigham Young noted that the ordinances performed in the Kirtland Temple were only "some of the first, or introductory, or initiatory ordinances, preparatory to an endowment." They were "but a faint similitude of the ordinances of the house of the Lord in their fulness."[19]

On 3 April 1836, Joseph Smith received several sets of keys from heavenly messengers inside the Kirtland Temple. Moses bestowed the keys of "gathering . . . Israel" (see D&C 110:11). The Prophet explained that "God gathers together the people in the last days to build unto the Lord a house to prepare them for the ordinances and endowment; washings and anointings, etc. . . . [including] baptism for the dead."[20] Elias committed "the gospel of Abraham" (D&C 110:12). This was called "Abraham's patriarchal power," "the priesthood of . . . Abraham," and "patriarchal authority."[21] The Prophet was specifically told in the Kirtland Temple that this power was connected with his "seed," or posterity (D&C 110:12). Since this same emphasis on one's "seed" can be found in the wording of the Abrahamic covenant (see Abraham 2:9–11), it can be concluded that Elias committed a power associated with marriage. The eternal nature and scope of this particular blessing can be seen by comparing Genesis 22:15–18 and D&C 132:30–31. Elijah appeared (in fulfillment of the prophecy that the angel had recited to Joseph Smith in 1823) and dispensed keys "to turn the hearts of the fathers to the children" (D&C 110:15). The Prophet clarified that "the word 'turn' here should be translated 'bind,' or 'seal'," and this all had to do with the Saints acting as "saviors on Mount Zion."[22] He further explained that to possess the power of Elijah was to "hold the keys of the revelations, ordinances, oracles, powers and endowments of the fullness of the Melchizedek Priesthood and of the kingdom of God on the earth and to receive, obtain and perform all the ordinances belonging to the kingdom of God . . . [which included] power . . . to seal those who dwell on earth to those which dwell in heaven."[23] Brigham Young taught that the Latter-day Saints were forced to leave Kirtland and its temple before the sanctuary could be "completed" with a font and the Nauvoo style of endowment given for the living and the dead.[24]

When the Prophet's father (Joseph Smith Sr.) gave patriarchal blessings inside of the Kirtland Temple in 1837, he made it clear that the Latter-day Saints were destined to become "kings and priests" in Zion.[25] During the 1830s, Father Smith taught in several of his blessings that Mount Zion was the name of the city of the Great King,[26] where a temple[27] with a veil[28] and a throne[29] would stand, and the Lord Jesus Christ would not only visit that holy structure,[30] but He would also administer the sacramental marriage supper to those who were present there.[31] Patriarch Smith further stated that the people on Mount Zion would be in a redeemed[32] and sanctified state,[33] would wear pure white robes,[34] would act in the capacity of saviors for others,[35] would be delivered or protected,[36] would have their identities recorded in the Book of Life,[37] would receive monikers that are mentioned in the book of Revelation,[38] and would be given an inheritance in conjunction with the covenant of the patriarchal fathers.[39]

The Lord gave a revelation through Joseph Smith on 26 April 1838 indicating that each member of the First Presidency would be shown the "pattern" for the Far West, Missouri Temple. The Lord cautioned that unless the temple was built according to this particular "pattern," He would not accept it (D&C 115:14–16). The question naturally arises as to why a new pattern for a temple would need to be given, since the Kirtland Temple had just recently been dedicated. A few months after the Lord spoke of the new pattern, one of the counselors in the First Presidency taught that "the object of our religion is to make us more intelligent than we could be without it." And in connection with the idea that the Far West Temple would be used for prayer, he said, "One part of the house shall be set apart for a place of worship, where we shall invoke our God for revelations . . . that by revelations, visions, etc. we may . . . . [obtain] that knowledge which is unto eternal life." Revelations that were expected to be gained inside of this sanctuary included information about the future of mankind, knowledge of "secrets and mysteries," and an understanding of Deities, angels, dominions, principalities, and powers.[40] In a letter written by the Prophet to the Church at large, in 1842, he said that the "keys of the kingdom" or "powers of the Holy Priesthood" that enable one to bind or seal on earth and in heaven—the keys of Elijah—enable the possessor to have "no difficulty in obtaining a knowledge of facts in relation to the salvation of the children of men, both as well for the dead as for the living"—the children/fathers aspect of the keys of Elijah (D&C 128:10–11; cf. 110:15).

In mid March 1839, the Prophet wrote in a letter, "I never have had [the] opportunity to give [the Saints] the plan that God has revealed to me,"[41] and later that year he taught one of the members of the Quorum of the Twelve Apostles "many great and glorious principles concerning God and the heavenly order of eternity," including the concepts of the "eternal union" of marriage and "eternal family organization."[42]

In September 1840, the First Presidency of the Church issued an epistle wherein they declared that the dispensation of the fullness of times would be an era when "all things" would be restored and the promises made to the fathers would be fulfilled. They said that they had been "given the pattern and design" for upbuilding God's kingdom on the earth and announced that the time had arrived for "establishing the Priesthood in their fullness and glory." They also indicated that it was time to build a temple in Nauvoo, and it would serve as a house of worship, prayer, and divinely established "ordinances."[43] At the October 1840 general conference of the Church, the Prophet discoursed on baptism for the dead one day and on the "plan of ordinances" that had been revealed to Adam or the "Ancient of Days" or "Michael" the next day. Some of the themes of this second sermon included premortal time, the creation, the Garden of Eden, and the Fall; the "keys" and "covenants" and power and glory with which God blessed Adam; the instructions, revelations, and commandments that the Lord gave to the first man; "the priesthood [being] restored with all its authority, power, and blessings" (i.e., in all its fullness) in the dispensation of the fullness of times, "every ordinance belonging to the priesthood" in "ancient days" being practiced within the Nauvoo Temple; priesthood "keys" that have been kept hidden; the mysteries of godliness; and certain kinds of sacrifice being made at an altar by latter-day sons of Levi (i.e., temple officiators) but after a pre-Mosaic or Melchizedekian type. All of this, said the Prophet, was "the order from the beginning" or the "order which [God] established . . . whereby He sent forth power, revelations, and glory."[44]

The First Presidency of the LDS Church printed an epistle on 15 January 1841 wherein they mentioned that the Nauvoo Temple would be "so constructed as to enable all the functions of the priesthood to be duly exercised, and where instructions from the Most High [would] be received." They also noted that the building of the temple would take great exertions, and so they requested the Saints to "freely make a sacrifice of their time, their talents, and their property, for the prosperity of the kingdom."[45]

On 19 January 1841, the Lord gave a revelation through Joseph Smith (see D&C 124) in which He provided information about the construction of a new sanctuary. The Lord commanded His Saints to build the Nauvoo Temple (see v. 31) because He desired to "reveal [His] ordinances therein unto [His] people," including "things which ha[d] been kept hid from before the foundation of the world" (vv. 40–41). The Lord used the same phraseology in teaching that He had "commanded" the building of the Mosaic tabernacle (where priestly initiations took place) and the Solomonic temple (where kingly initiations took place) so that "those ordinances might be revealed which had been hid from before the world was" (v. 38). Thus, there would be a direct connection between the rituals of the temples of ancient Israel and the temple in Nauvoo, Illinois. The Lord further stated that He would "show unto [His] servant Joseph [Smith] all things pertaining to this house, and the priesthood thereof" (v. 42), and He also indicated that the purpose of building the house was so that He could "restore again that which was lost . . . even the fulness of the priesthood" (v. 28).[46] The Lord even listed some of the activities that would take place inside His latter-day house. They included baptism for the dead, washings, anointings, solemn assemblies (cf. Ezek. 44:24), statutes (i.e., laws) and judgments (cf. 1 Kgs. 6:12), keys to "ask and receive" (cf. Matt. 21:22),[47] memorials of sacrifices by the sons of Levi, and conversations and oracles (i.e., revelations) in "most holy places" (vv. 39, 95, 97; cf. 1 Kgs. 6:16). All of this would serve to bestow "glory, honor, and endowment"[48] upon temple patrons and lay the "foundation of Zion" (v. 39).

On 6 April 1841, a person who was not a Latter-day Saint witnessed the cornerstone laying ceremony for the Nauvoo Temple and reported the following in a newspaper: "It [has] been 'revealed' to Jo[seph] Smith . . . that a temple must be built at this place, and the dimensions, architecture, arrangement, and devotions hav[e] all been prescribed with no less minuteness than were those of the ancient Jewish sanctuary."[49]

William W. Phelps wrote in June 1841 that he had learned from Hyrum Smith (the Prophet's brother) that "the Lord ha[d] revealed something relative to the fulness of the priesthood, or

in other words, new things relating to that sacred order." Brother
Phelps said that he would "drop a few hints" about the matter
and proceeded to give a short discourse on prayer—which
he called "the sacred coin of the heart which buys blessings"
(cf. D&C 124:95, 97). He ended his letter by quoting from
a section of the book of Revelation that speaks of "kings and
priests" who hold containers of incense in the heavenly temple;
the smoke of the incense representing the prayers of the Saints
(Rev. 5:6–10; cf. 8:3–4).[50]

On 12 October 1841, the Quorum of the Twelve Apostles
printed a letter in which they indicated that the Nauvoo Temple
would be a place for proxy baptism, worship, endowment,
the revelation of God's laws, and the manifestation of "all the
ordinances."[51] On 15 November 1841, the Apostles published
another epistle wherein they stated that the Nauvoo Temple
would be a place of instruction and endowment with power. "In
this house," they said, "all the ordinances will be made manifest,
and many things will be shown forth, which have been hid from
generation to generation."[52] One of the Saints who arrived in
Nauvoo at the very end of the year reported, "In this temple
built by divine command, I am informed we are to have made
known to us the fulness of the priesthood."[53]

The Prophet published the first installment of the book of
Abraham in the 1 March 1842 edition of the *Times and Seasons*
(though there is evidence that some of this material had already
been produced by 1837). Some of the themes in this section
of the book included the creation, priesthood and kingship,
heirship, the order of Adam, obedience, sacrifice and prayer at
an altar, the right of the firstborn, divine protection, receiving
instructions and greater knowledge, entering the Lord's presence, and eternal life.[54]

On 4 March 1842, Reuben Hedlock met with Joseph Smith
at the latter's redbrick store office and was shown the original
Egyptian hypocephalus known as facsimile #2 of the book

of Abraham. The Prophet gave Brother Hedlock instructions concerning "the arrangement of the writing" that he needed to engrave on a woodblock along with a number-coded image of the circular Egyptian diagram.[55] Some of the themes associated with the facsimile writings were as follows: the celestial residence of God; the creation; the sun, moon, stars, and earth; Adam in the Garden of Eden, offering sacrifice at an altar; kingship; priesthood; the holy temple; hidden knowledge; God revealing keywords through the heavens;[56] and being clothed with power, authority, and light.

By examining all of the above timeline items, it becomes obvious that the Nauvoo-era temple ordinances and doctrines did not suspiciously materialize after Joseph Smith became a Freemason. It can be plainly seen that the Lord was involved in the restoration of the fullness of temple activities from the outset of the latter-day dispensation (see JS—H 1:30–41). He not only taught His Prophet the concepts of temple worship (see D&C 84), but He also sent His representatives to bestow keys of accomplishment on Joseph Smith (see D&C 110), and then He listed the ritual activities that would take place inside of His holy house (see D&C 124)—all before the Prophet was taught the mysteries of Masonry.

NOTES

1. The angel "quoted the second chapter of Joel from the twenty-eighth to the last verse" (*Times and Seasons,* vol. 3, no. 12, 15 April 1842, 753; hereafter cited as *T&S*).

2. See *Messenger and Advocate,* vol. 1, no. 7, April 1835, 112; hereafter cited as *M&A*.

3. Since the Lord specified in this scriptural passage that the Aaronic priests were to be washed, anointed, and clothed in "holy garments" before serving in the temple, the same requirements would naturally apply to those who received the same priesthood in the latter days—though these requirements were not fully implemented until the Nauvoo period of Church history.

4. *T&S,* vol. 3, no. 19, 1 August 1842, 865–66.

5. *M&A,* vol. 1, no. 1, October 1834, 16.

6. See *T&S,* vol. 3, no. 19, 1 August 1842, 866; Brigham H. Roberts, ed., *History of the Church* (Salt Lake City: Deseret News Press, 1930), 1:40; hereafter cited as *HC*.

7. Parley P. Pratt, *Autobiography of Parley P. Pratt,* rev. ed. (Salt Lake City: Deseret Book, 2000), 42.

8. *HC,* 2:309.

9. Kate B. Carter, comp., *Our Pioneer Heritage* (Salt Lake City: Daughters of Utah Pioneers, 1967), 10:198.

10. *Juvenile Instructor,* vol. 27, no. 3, 1 February 1892, 93. There are other instances in Church history of angels being seen in this type of clothing before March 1842.

11. *Evening and Morning Star,* vol. 2, no. 18, March 1834, 144.

12. See *Lectures on Faith* (Salt Lake City: Deseret Book, 1985), 1–83.

13. William Draper autobiography, 2, L. Tom Perry Special Collections, Harold B. Lee Library, Brigham Young University, Provo, Utah.

14. *M&A,* vol. 1, no. 9, June 1835, 130.

15. Emma Smith, comp., *A Collection of Sacred Hymns for the Church of the Latter Day Saints* (Kirtland, OH: Frederick G. Williams and Company, 1835), 81–82.

16. *Brigham Young University Studies,* vol. 12, no. 4, Summer 1972, 416.

17. Ibid., 419.

18. See Dean C. Jessee, ed., *Personal Writings of Joseph Smith,* rev. ed. (Salt Lake City and Provo, UT: Deseret Book and Brigham Young University Press, 2004), 175; hereafter cited as *PWJS; Woman's Exponent,* vol. 9, no. 17, 1 February 1881, 130; George D. Watt, ed., *Journal of Discourses* (Liverpool, England: Franklin D. and Samuel W. Richards, 1854–1886), 9:41; hereafter cited as *JD.*

19. Ibid., 2:31.

20. Andrew F. Ehat and Lyndon W. Cook, eds., *The Words of Joseph Smith: The Contemporary Accounts of the Nauvoo Discourses of the Prophet Joseph* (Orem, UT: Grandin Book, 1991), 213; hereafter cited as *WJS.*

21. Ibid., 245–46.

22. *HC,* 6:183–84.

23. *WJS,* 329. President John Taylor stated that "unless Elijah had come and conferred the keys, it would not have been revealed" how to "administer" in Latter-day Saint temples of the post-Kirtland period (*JD,* 26:109).

24. Ibid., 2:32, 18:305.

25. H. Michael Marquardt, comp., *Early Patriarchal Blessings of The Church of Jesus Christ of Latter-day Saints* (Salt Lake City: The Smith-Pettit Foundation, 2007), 158, 160, 168–69.

26. See ibid., 130, 144.

27. See ibid., 50, 83, 88, 92, 124, 143, 154, 178, 182.

28. See ibid., 87, 153, 182.

29. See ibid., 124.

30. See ibid., 107, 129–30, 178.

31. See ibid., 130, 175.

32. See ibid., 147.

33. See ibid., 32, 175.

34. See ibid., 68, 77, 109, 116.

35. See ibid., 89, 151, 177.

36. See ibid., 94, 130.

37. See ibid., 139.

38. See ibid., 139, 176, 189.

39. See ibid., 153.

40. *Oration Delivered by Mr. S[idney] Rigdon on the 4th of July, 1838* (Far West, MO: Elders' Journal Office, 1838), 9–10.

41. *PWJS*, 427.

42. Parley P. Pratt, *Autobiography of Parley P. Pratt*, rev. ed. (Salt Lake City: Deseret Book, 2000), 361.

43. *T&S*, vol. 1, no. 12, October 1840, 178–79.

44. *WJS*, 38–44.

45. *T&S*, vol. 2, no. 6, 15 January 1841, 274, 277.

46. Parley P. Pratt taught that in order for a person to be perfected in the fullness of the priesthood, they needed to receive "holy washings, anointings, keys, ordinances, oracles and instructions" (Parley P. Pratt, *Key to the Science of Theology* [Liverpool: F. D. Richards, 1855], 90). Another definition was given by Brigham Young on 6 August 1843: "For any person to have the fulness of [the Melchizedek] priesthood, he must be a king and priest" (*HC*, 5:527). Joseph Smith said on 27 August 1843, "Those holding the fulness of the Melchizedek Priesthood are kings and priests of the Most High God" (ibid., 5:555). Orson Hyde taught that "the fulness of the priesthood includes the authority of both king and priest" (*Millennial Star*, vol. 9, no. 2, 15 January 1847, 23).

47. Under the editorship of Apostle John Taylor, the Church's newspaper in Nauvoo printed a short article which said that "prayer" was among the "ordinances" of the temple (*T&S*, vol. 6, no. 18, 1 December 1845, 1050). Compare this with Elder Orson Pratt's published footnotes for Doctrine and

Covenants 124:95, 97 (*The Doctrine and Covenants* [Salt Lake City: George Q. Cannon and Sons, 1891], 441 ns. 2o and 2p).

48. This phrase is interesting because the "holy garments" or temple clothing of ancient Israel was designed to bestow glory and beauty on the wearer (Ex. 28:2, 40) but the Hebrew word translated as "beauty" (*tiph'arah*) is rendered elsewhere in the Old Testament as "honor" (Deut. 26:19; Jgs. 4:9; Ps. 71:8). The Greek word translated as 'endow' or 'endowment' (*enduo*) means to put on clothing.

49. *Pittsburgh Christian Advocate,* vol. 8, no. 28, 23 June 1841.

50. *T&S,* vol. 2, no. 16, 15 June 1841, 451.

51. Ibid., vol. 2, no. 24, 15 October 1841, 569.

52. Ibid., vol. 3, no. 2, 15 November 1841, 601.

53. Ibid., vol. 3, no. 5, 1 January 1842, 648–49.

54. See ibid., vol. 3, no. 9, 1 March 1842, 704–706.

55. *HC,* 4:543.

56. It is interesting to note that there were stars embroidered on the veil which concealed the Holy Place of the Jerusalem Temple (see William Whiston, trans., *Josephus: Complete Works* [Grand Rapids, MI: Kregel, 1960], 555).

CHAPTER 6

A Provisional Temple

The construction of the Nauvoo Temple was formally announced in a First Presidency letter[1] written in September 1840. Also, during a session of the LDS Church's general conference on 3 October 1840, the Prophet made a public declaration of the same.[2] About three and a half months later, the Lord gave a revelation wherein He explained the type of ordinances that would take place inside that structure (see D&C 124:39). Yet, this building would not receive a capstone[3] until 24 May 1845, and the interior would not be finished to the point where endowments could be given until December 10th[4] of that same year—one and a half years after Joseph Smith had died.

There is some evidence that the Prophet knew he would not live to be forty years of age, with several historical records verifying that he felt he must hasten to finish his assignment of establishing the dispensation of the fullness of times.[5] President John Taylor described the course of action that Joseph Smith took because of the latter's feelings of apprehension. He said,

> Joseph Smith before his death was much exercised about the completion of the temple in Nauvoo and the administering of ordinances therein. In his anxiety, and for fear he should not live to see the temple completed, he prepared a place over what was known as the brick store . . . where, to a chosen few, he administered those ordinances that we now have today associated with endowments, so that if anything should happen to him—which he evidently contemplated—he would feel that he had then fulfilled his mission, that he had

conferred upon others all the keys given to him by the manifestations of the power of God.[6]

The Prophet's redbrick store, mentioned by President Taylor, was a fairly new edifice. It had been completed in late 1841 and was opened for business as a mercantile establishment on 5 January 1842.[7] This structure had three levels: a cellar, a depot, and a loft. The uppermost story consisted of an open space that measured approximately 44 x 25 feet in size. It was painted white in color and had three large rectangular windows on its northern wall.[8] Another window was located in the Prophet's small office, which was situated against the south edge of the building.[9]

Lucius Scovil reminisced during the Utah period of Church history that on 3 May 1842, Joseph Smith summoned Scovil and a few other men to the top floor of his store. The Prophet informed these individuals that his objective was to "fit up that room preparatory to giving endowments to a few Elders." The Church President gave continual directions on what needed to be done, and before noon on May 4th, "everything was arranged representing the interior of a temple as much as the circumstances would permit."[10] Brigham Young (one of the few people who received the temple rituals on the 4th) recalled that the hall was divided up into several different departments.[11] One of the workmen who helped to furnish these rooms said that "trees" were placed in one of them in order to represent a "garden."[12]

THE PARTICIPANTS

There were nine people who received the temple endowment from the Prophet Joseph Smith on 4 May 1842. These individuals were James Adams, Hyrum Smith, Newel K. Whitney, George Miller, Brigham Young, Heber C. Kimball, Willard Richards,[13] William Marks and William Law.[14]

A question naturally arises after perusing this list of nine names. Why were these particular men[15] chosen as the first individuals to receive the Nauvoo-era temple ordinances? One possible explanation presents itself by examining the temple-related revelation now known as D&C 124 (given 19 January 1841). Nearly all of the recipients of the ordinances on 4 May 1842 were mentioned in this set of instructions from the Lord (Newel K. Whitney and James Adams being the exceptions). Indeed, the Lord specifically commanded Joseph Smith in this revelation to give two of those named—Hyrum Smith and William Law—specific elements of the endowment (vv. 95, 97).¹⁶ It is, therefore, possible that seven of the nine men were chosen to participate because they were named in the Nauvoo Temple revelation.

The following short biographies of the inaugural endowment participants will name them in the order of their appearance in Doctrine and Covenants 124, list any other temple connections that they had, describe the various ecclesiastical positions that they held in the LDS Church at the time, and make note of their Masonic backgrounds when they administered and received the temple ordinances.

Joseph Smith is identified as the Lord's "servant" in the first verse of section 124 of the Doctrine and Covenants and is confirmed as presiding elder, prophet, seer, revelator, and translator in verse 125. In verse 42 of this same revelation, the Lord promises to show Joseph Smith "all thing pertaining to [the Nauvoo Temple], and the priesthood thereof." And in verses 95 and 97, the Lord directs President Smith to bestow certain endowment elements upon specific individuals. The Prophet had previously directed the building and dedication efforts of the Independence, Missouri, and Kirtland, Ohio, temples (see D&C 109), and he both received and administered the rituals of the Kirtland Temple.¹⁷ He later received authority, knowledge, and power pertaining to the Nauvoo-era temple ordinances while inside the Kirtland sanctuary (see D&C 110). Joseph Smith was taken through the three degrees of York Masonry in quick succession on the 15th and 16th of March 1842. On these occasions, Hyrum Smith, Newel K. Whitney, and Heber C. Kimball were present, and all three had officiating duties assigned to them at the time.[18]

Hyrum Smith is first mentioned in verse 15 of D&C 124. He is assigned as Co-President of the Church in verses 94 through 96 and also as the Presiding Patriarch of the Church in verses 91 through 93. He was told by the Lord that he would "hold the sealing blessings of [the] church, even the Holy Spirit of promise, whereby [the Saints] are sealed up unto the day of redemption" (v. 124), and he was also informed that his brother Joseph Smith would show him elements of the temple ceremonies (v. 95). Hyrum had helped to begin the construction of the Kirtland Temple, lay its cornerstones, and supervise the building of it.[19] He was also present during its dedication services.[20] He both received and administered the Kirtland-era temple ordinances.[21] Hyrum had acted as a proxy for baptism in the font of the Nauvoo Temple in late 1841.[22] He had been initiated into the three basic degrees of Freemasonry while his family was residing in New York state,[23] and he acted in two officiating capacities within the Nauvoo Lodge.[24] He also served in a standing administrative role of that same lodge[25] before he received the 1842 endowment.

George Miller was confirmed in the bishopric in D&C 124:20–21. He was likely one of "the Bishops" who participated in laying one of the Nauvoo Temple cornerstones which was "expressive of the Lesser Priesthood."[26] He had become a Freemason in the state of Virginia[27] about the year 1819[28] and was assigned by Grand Master Abraham Jonas to be the first administrative Master of the Nauvoo Lodge.[29]

William Marks was assigned to ordain and bless one of the Lord's servants in D&C 124:79. He was serving as a stake president in Nauvoo, Illinois, when he received the endowment.[30] It was reported in the *Times and Seasons* newspaper that he had assisted in laying one of the cornerstones of the Nauvoo Temple.[31] He was initiated as a Master Mason on 22 April 1842 with Hyrum Smith and George Miller present and officiating.[32]

William Law was assigned as the second counselor in the First Presidency of The Church of Jesus Christ of Latter-day Saints in D&C 124:126, and it was specified in this same revelation that he was to learn of certain endowment-related items from Joseph Smith (see v. 97). The Nauvoo Lodge records indicate that he became a Master Mason on 27 April 1842 with Hyrum Smith presiding and George Miller and Willard Richards present.[33]

Brigham Young was assigned to act as President of the Quorum of the Twelve Apostles in Doctrine and Covenants 124:127. He had previously worked on the completion of the Kirtland Temple,[34] attended its dedication,[35] and also received the endowment rituals that were given there to priesthood holders.[36] On 21 November 1841, he assisted in baptizing proxies inside of the Nauvoo Temple.[37] Elder Young had been raised to the degree of Master Mason in the Nauvoo Lodge on 9 April 1842, with Joseph Smith and Willard Richards present (Richards being initiated) and Hyrum Smith, Newel K. Whitney, and Heber C. Kimball each officiating.[38]

Heber C. Kimball was confirmed as a member of the Quorum of the Twelve Apostles in D&C 124:129. He had been initiated into the three fundamental degrees of Freemasonry in the state of New York in 1823[39] and believed that the world would be a much better place if men everywhere lived up to the high moral and ethical standards of the Craft.[40] He had previously received the endowment of the Kirtland era[41] and attended the dedication of the Kirtland Temple.[42] In addition, he had officiated in performing proxy baptisms inside the Nauvoo Temple in 1841.[43] Brother Kimball served in two administrative roles for the Nauvoo Lodge[44] and was serving in an officiating capacity on the days when Joseph Smith was inducted into the Masonic fraternity.[45]

Willard Richards was confirmed as a member of the Quorum of the Twelve Apostles in D&C 124:129. He had been appointed on 13 December 1841 to act in the roles of Joseph Smith's personal scribe and the Nauvoo Temple recorder (the latter station may explain his presence during the bestowal of the first temple ordinances).[46] Richards had confirmed individuals after they had been baptized by proxy for the dead in the Nauvoo Temple's font.[47] He was initiated as a Master Mason in the Nauvoo Lodge on 9 April 1842 with Joseph Smith and Brigham Young present (Young being initiated) and Hyrum Smith, Newel K. Whitney, and Heber C. Kimball each officiating.[48]

Newel K. Whitney was not mentioned in Doctrine and Covenants 124. However, the Lord had formerly linked him to the building of the Kirtland Temple in 1833 (see D&C 96:2), and he was one of the twenty-four persons who laid that building's cornerstones.[49] He also had worked on the construction of the Kirtland Temple, was present at its dedication,[50] and received the endowment ordinances associated with that building.[51] At the time he received the Nauvoo endowment, he was a traveling or general bishop of the Church,[52] and in that capacity he had dedicated one of the cornerstones of the Nauvoo Temple in April 1841. This particular cornerstone was, in his own words, "expressive of the Lesser [or Aaronic] Priesthood."[53] He had become a Freemason long before while residing in the state of Ohio,[54] was present when the first meeting of Mormon Masons accepted a dispensation to form a lodge at the end of December 1841,[55] and served in a standing administrative role within that Masonic unit.[56]

James Adams was another person who was not mentioned in section 124 of the Doctrine and Covenants. He was a relatively recent convert to the LDS Church and was serving as a branch president in Springfield, Illinois, when the endowment was first given.[57] He had traveled to Nauvoo on 30 April 1842 and spent most of that day with Joseph Smith.[58] He stayed in Nauvoo for several more days during which the Prophet discoursed upon the temple and its ordinances.[59] He then returned to Springfield immediately after receiving the temple ordinances.[60] This information suggests that James Adams may have been included in the first endowment group simply because he happened to be in Nauvoo at the right time and the Prophet considered him to be a close friend.[61] Brother Adams had served as the Master of the Freemasons lodge in Springfield, Illinois,[62] and he was elected to the office of Deputy Grand Master of the Grand Lodge of Illinois in 1840—holding that status on the day he received the Nauvoo endowment.[63]

THE EXPERIENCE

Between 14th and 18th April 1845, Apostle Willard Richard penned a summary of what the nine men had experienced in the upper room of the redbrick store three years earlier.[64] This summation was first printed—as part of the Church's serial history project—in the *Deseret News*[65] and was eventually included at the beginning of volume five of the *History of the Church*. Elder Richards's notes are important because they provide a glimpse of the event from an eyewitness perspective and also give the reader a sanctioned report on the character and content of the temple ordinances. Elder Richards indicated that these ordinances were not elitist—they were meant to be "made known to all the Saints" who had "prepared" themselves. He specifically stated that the things they would receive would be of a "spiritual" nature and needed to be experienced inside the sacred space of the Nauvoo Temple. With regard to the teachings and ordinances involved, Apostle Richards wrote that the Prophet Joseph Smith instructed the first full endowment recipients in the principles and order of the Priesthood, attending to washings, anointings, endowments and the communication of keys pertaining to the Aaronic Priesthood, and so on to the highest order of the Melchizedek Priesthood, setting forth the order pertaining to the Ancient of Days, and all those plans and principles by which anyone is enabled to secure the fullness of those blessings which have been prepared for the Church of the Firstborn, and come up and abide in the presence of the Eloheim in the eternal worlds. In this council was instituted the ancient order of things for the first time in these last days.[66]

It should be noted that Elder Richards labeled these proceedings as "the ancient order of things" and also "the order pertaining to the Ancient of Days." Since in Latter-day Saint terminology the Ancient of Days is Michael the Archangel or Adam (see D&C 27:11, 107:54, 128:21), it can be deduced that the LDS temple ordinances were viewed by the Nauvoo Saints as descending from the time of the first human interaction with God. The Prophet was publicly teaching this primordial backdrop for the Nauvoo Temple ceremonies as early as 5 October 1840—seventeen months before he became a Freemason.

When the temple in St. George, Utah, was dedicated by President Brigham Young in 1877, he reminisced about when he had first received the temple ordinances back in 1842. He explained that after Joseph Smith had given the inaugural group the various elements that constituted the endowment, he turned to him (Brigham Young) and gave him an administrative task. He said, "Brother Brigham, this is not arranged right but we have done the best we could under the circumstances in which we are placed and I wish you to take this matter in hand and organize and systematize all these ceremonies." President Young confirmed that he performed this duty and each time the endowment was performed before the completion of the Nauvoo Temple, he "got something more" out of what he saw and subsequently "understood . . . how to place" things inside the larger building when it was finished.[67] His chore of comprehension and systemization began the day after he received the ordinances. The entry for 5 May 1842 in the *History of the Church* reports that on that day, James Adams returned to Springfield, Illinois, while the remaining brethren acted as officiators in giving Joseph Smith and his brother Hyrum the endowment.[68]

THE REACTION

Nine men who were Freemasons received the Nauvoo temple endowment from a man who was also a Freemason. And there was no mistaking that there were some resemblances between the two rituals for, as Heber C. Kimball wrote just a month after being endowed, "There is a similarity of Priesthood in Masonry."[69] And yet, no incredulous cry about bootlegging or fraud rang out from this group against the Prophet. In fact, all of the long-term Masons among them acted in just the opposite manner. A survey of their post-endowment activities and attitudes is most instructive.

On 27 May 1842, Newel K. Whitney spoke to a gathering of the Nauvoo Relief Society sisters—the Prophet being present—and he hinted at the "astonishment" he felt about the "great blessings" of the temple. Like Heber C. Kimball, he spoke of "precious"[70] things of the "Priesthood" that caused him to "rejoice" and, like Hyrum Smith, he spoke of the "power" and "intelligence" to be gained through the temple ceremonies.[71] During the next month, he and six other members of the inaugural temple group met with the Prophet in order to attend to temple matters.[72] The following year, Bishop Whitney received temple ordinance instructions from the Prophet,[73] and a few years later he acted as an ordinance worker on the first day the endowment was given to the Saints inside of the Nauvoo Temple.[74]

In a letter to a fellow Apostle dated 17 June 1842, Heber C. Kimball referred to the temple ordinances as "precious things . . . on the Priesthood that would cause your soul to rejoice."[75] Just a few days later, Elder Kimball met with Joseph Smith and six other members of the first endowment group to engage in temple-related business.[76] Then in a public address delivered on 8 April 1845, he stated that the "ordinances of the House of God" were "necessary" things for the Saints to receive and that obtaining them would have the effect of upsetting Satan.[77] Elder Kimball received temple ordinance instructions from Joseph Smith one year after initially receiving the ceremonies,[78] and he was engaged as an ordinance worker on the first day that the endowment was given to the Saints inside the Nauvoo sanctuary.[79]

In June 1842, Hyrum Smith met with the Prophet and six other members of the endowment group in order to conduct temple-related business.[80] In late May of 1843, Hyrum sat in council with some of the members of the first endowment group in order to receive more instructions on temple matters from his brother.[81] At the general conference of the Church in April 1844, Hyrum Smith declared from the stand, "I cannot make a comparison between the house of God and anything now in existence. Great things are to grow out of that house; there is a great and mighty power to grow out of it; there is an endowment; knowledge is power, we want knowledge."[82] It is known from the historical record that Hyrum continued to participate in temple-related activities while the Nauvoo Temple was being built.[83]

After James Adams received the temple ordinances, he acted as an agent for the Church's newspaper in Springfield, Illinois,[84] he sold land to the Church,[85] and he sat in ecclesiastical council with the Church's top leadership.[86] Brother Adams continued to participate in temple-centered activities,[87] and he intended to move to Nauvoo, Illinois shortly before his death in the summer of 1843.[88]

The month after bishop George Miller was endowed, he met with Joseph Smith and six other members of the first Nauvoo temple group to participate in temple-related activity.[89] On 15 January 1845, bishop Miller signed his name to a public announcement wherein he expressed his anxiety that the Saints construct the Nauvoo Temple as speedily as possible so that they might receive the "reward" of the endowment.[90] At the beginning of February 1845, he again proclaimed that he felt "very anxious to have the temple finished immediately."[91] He was engaged as an ordinance administrator on the first day that the endowment was given to the Saints inside of the Nauvoo Temple.[92]

The reaction of the short-term Freemasons who attended the first Nauvoo endowment session is also worthy of note. On 26 June 1842, Willard Richards, Brigham Young, and William Marks met with Joseph Smith and four of the long-term Freemasons from the group and participated in temple-related functions.[93] On 26 May 1843, Brigham Young, Willard Richards, and William Law met in the upper room of the redbrick store with four of the long-term Freemasons from the inaugural temple group and received instructions from Joseph Smith on the priesthood, endowments, and the new and ever-lasting covenant.[94]

It should further be noted that when temple work began for the general Church populace in the Nauvoo Temple on 10 December 1845, Brigham Young, Willard Richards, George Miller, Heber C. Kimball, and Newel K. Whitney were each present and acting in various administrative and participatory roles.[95]

NOTES

1. See *Times and Seasons,* vol. 1, no. 12, October 1840, 178–79; hereafter cited as *T&S.*

2. See ibid., vol. 1, no. 12, October 1840, 186.

3. See *Brigham Young University Studies,* vol. 19, no. 3, Spring 1979, 311; hereafter cited as *BYUS.*

4. See ibid., vol. 34, no. 2, 1994–95, 22.

5. See *BYUS,* vol. 21, no. 3, Summer 1981, 306–307. Wilford Woodruff quoted the Prophet as saying, "I have desired to see [the Nauvoo] Temple built, but I shall not live to see it" (George D. Watt, ed., *Journal of Discourses* [Liverpool: Franklin D. and Samuel W. Richards, 1854–1886], 13:164; hereafter cited as *JD*).

6. Ibid., 25:183.

7. See Brigham H. Roberts, ed., *History of the Church* (Salt Lake City: Deseret News Press, 1930), 4:491; hereafter cited as *HC.*

8. See *BYUS,* vol. 19, no. 3, Spring 1979, 363.

9. See *HC,* 4:491.

10. *Deseret News Semi Weekly,* vol. 9, no. 3, 15 February 1884, 2. Lucius N. Scovil had been a long-term Freemason and one of the signatories on the petition to establish a Masonic lodge at Nauvoo. His reaction to the temple rituals bears repeating. He heard comments by the Prophet during the two days of preparation and recalled, "He gave us many items [of instruction] that were very interesting to us, which sank with deep weight upon my mind, especially after the temple was finished at Nauvoo, and I received the ordinances" (ibid.).

11. L. John Nuttal dairy, 7 February 1877, L. Tom Perry Special Collections, Harold B. Lee Library, Brigham Young University, Provo, Utah.

12. Dimick B. Huntington statement, 12 December 1878 in Devery S. Anderson and Gary J. Bergera, eds., *Joseph Smith's*

Quorum of the Anointed (Salt Lake City: Signature Books, 2005), 3. Twenty-five to thirty potted evergreens were placed in the Nauvoo Temple's garden room (see *BYUS*, vol. 15, no. 4, Summer 1975, 476). The garden room located in some Latter-day Saint temples is mentioned in the *Ensign*, July 1977, photos; ibid., October 1988, 35–36; ibid., March 1993, photo; ibid., February 1995, photo; *New Era*, January 1994, 17.

13. See *HC,* 5:1–2.

14. The last two persons on the list are referred to in Dean C. Jessee, ed., *The Papers of Joseph Smith* (Salt Lake City: Deseret Book, 1992), 2:380, Donald W. Parry, ed., *Temples of the Ancient World: Ritual and Symbolism* (Salt Lake City: Deseret Book, 1994), 50, and *BYUS*, vol. 22, no. 1, Winter 1982, 54 n. 28.

15. A little more than thirty days before Joseph Smith first gave the endowment to men, he indicated that women would receive it also. On 30 March 1842 the Prophet said that the Relief Society was going to become "a kingdom of priests" as in ancient days (Andrew F. Ehat and Lyndon W. Cook, eds., *The Words of Joseph Smith: The Contemporary Accounts of the Nauvoo Discourses of the Prophet Joseph,* rev. ed. [Orem, UT: Grandin Books, 1991], 110; hereafter cited as *WJS*). When a synopsis of these remarks was entered into the *History of the Church* it was clarified that "the Lord was going to make of the Church of Jesus Christ a kingdom of Priests" (*HC,* 4:570; cf. Ex. 19:6)—thus, the remark pertained to both the men and the women of the Church. At the 28 April 1842 meeting of the Relief Society the Prophet stated that he intended to give specific endowment elements to members of that group (*WJS,* 116). In the *History of the Church* text related to this same meeting Apostle George A. Smith clarified (as editor) that the women would receive these blessings "in connection with their husbands" (*HC,* 4:604). On 27 May 1842, Newel K. Whitney—with the Prophet present—told the Relief Society sisters that "the intent of the[ir] society" was to help "fully restore the Priesthood" or, in other words,

receive "certain blessings" that God had bestowed upon Adam and Eve. These blessings, he said, would be given to them "in connection with their husbands" (*Woman's Exponent*, vol. 20, no. 19, 15 April 1892, 149). It appears that Joseph Smith would have endowed women along with the men on 4 May 1842 but he wanted his wife, Emma Smith, to be the first woman to receive the ordinances (thereafter to act as an officiator for other women), and she did not receive them until one year later (see Lyndon W. Cook, *The Revelations of the Prophet Joseph Smith* [Salt Lake City: Deseret Book, 1985], 293–94; hereafter cited as *RPJS*).

16. See Elder Orson Pratt's statements in *The Doctrine and Covenants* (Salt Lake City: George Q. Cannon and Sons, 1891), 441 ns. 2o and 2p.

17. See *HC*, 2:379, 382, 430.

18. See Mervin B. Hogan, *The Founding Minutes of Nauvoo Lodge* (Des Moines, IA: Research Lodge Number, 1971), 11–13.

19. See *HC*, 1:353; D&C 94:14–15; article on the Kirtland Temple cornerstones (*Church News*, 17 July 1993, 5).

20. See *HC*, 2:411.

21. See ibid., 2:379, 382, 430.

22. See *BYUS*, vol. 32, nos. 1–2, Winter and Spring 1992, 51.

23. See Hogan, *The Founding Minutes of Nauvoo Lodge*, 8.

24. See ibid., 9, 15.

25. See ibid., 7.

26. *T&S*, vol. 2, no. 12, 15 April 1841, 377.

27. See Hogan, *The Founding Minutes of Nauvoo Lodge*, 8.

28. See *BYUS*, vol. 19, no. 3, Spring 1979, 403 n. 1.

29. Hogan, *The Founding Minutes of Nauvoo Lodge*, 3.

30. See Glen M. Leonard, *Nauvoo: A Place of Peace, A People of Promise* (Salt Lake City and Provo, UT: Deseret Book and BYU Press, 2002), 704 n. 107.

31. See *T&S*, vol. 2, no. 12, 15 April 1841, 377.

32. See Hogan, *The Founding Minutes of Nauvoo Lodge*, 23–24.

33. See ibid., 25–26.

34. See *HC*, 2:399.

35. See *RPJS*, 279.

36. See Susan Easton Black and Larry C. Porter, eds., *Lion of the Lord: Essays on the Life and Service of Brigham Young* (Salt Lake City: Deseret Book, 1995), 110.

37. See *HC*, 4:454.

38. See Hogan, *The Founding Minutes of Nauvoo Lodge*, 15–16.

39. See Orson F. Whitney, *Life of Heber C. Kimball* (Salt Lake City: Juvenile Instructor Office, 1888), 26; Hogan, *The Founding Minutes of Nauvoo Lodge*, 8.

40. See Whitney, *Life of Heber C. Kimball*, 27.

41. See *BYUS*, vol. 15, no. 4, Summer 1975, 459.

42. See *RPJS*, 264.

43. See *HC*, 4:454.

44. See Hogan, *The Founding Minutes of Nauvoo Lodge*, 4, 7.

45. See ibid., 11, 13.

46. See *HC*, 4:470; *T&S*, vol. 3, no. 4, 15 December 1841, 638.

47. See *HC*, 4:454.

48. See Hogan, *The Founding Minutes of Nauvoo Lodge*, 15–16.

49. See the article on the laying of the Kirtland Temple cornerstones in *Church News*, 17 July 1993, 5.

50. See *RPJS*, 103.

51. See *HC*, 2:381–82, 391, 430.

52. See *JD*, 22:34–35.

53. *T&S*, vol. 2, no. 12, 15 April 1841, 377.

54. See Hogan, *The Founding Minutes of Nauvoo Lodge*, 9.

55. See ibid., 4.

56. See ibid., 7.

57. Leonard, *Nauvoo: A Place of Peace, A People of Promise,* 704 n. 107.

58. See *HC,* 4:608.

59. See ibid.

60. See *HC,* 5:2.

61. See ibid., 6:51.

62. See Kent L. Walgren, "James Adams: Early Springfield Mormon and Freemason," *Journal of the Illinois State Historical Society,* vol. 75, no. 2, Summer 1982, 125–27.

63. See Dean C. Jessee, ed., *The Papers of Joseph Smith* (Salt Lake City: Deseret Book, 1992), 2:521.

64. See *BYUS,* vol. 11, no. 4, Summer 1971, 467.

65. See *Deseret News,* vol. 5, no. 29, 26 September 1855, 1.

66. *HC,* 5:2. The Prophet Joseph Smith taught that these ordinances were not optional but were necessary for persons who desired to obtain "celestial thrones" (ibid., 6:319) or, in other words, receive the "fullness of salvation" (ibid., 6:184).

67. *BYUS,* vol. 19, no. 2, Winter 1979, 159 n. 77. Since Joseph Smith gave Brigham Young latitude in fine-tuning the things he had taught the nine men on 4 May 1842 the student of history is left with the question of what exactly it was that the Prophet initially bequeathed to the group and what amendments may have subsequently taken place at the instigation of, or with the approval of, Brigham Young.

68. See *HC,* 5:2–3. Hyrum probably received the endowment again (along with Joseph) because he was the Co-President of the Church. The pattern for this sequence of action can be seen in the inaugural baptisms of the final gospel dispensation. Joseph Smith received authority to baptize, then he administered the ordinance, then he received the ordinance. Joseph received authority to conduct the Nauvoo-era endowment while in the Kirtland Temple (see D&C 110), then he administered the ordinance, then he received the ordinance.

69. *BYUS,* vol. 19, no. 2, Winter 1979, 145 n. 26. Heber

C. Kimball's statement naturally raises the question of the meaning behind the similarities that exist between the rituals of Mormonism and Masonry. An article published in the *Encyclopedia of Mormonism* addresses how some Latter-day Saints have come to view this issue. It says, "Students of both Mormonism and Freemasonry have pondered possible relationships between Masonic rites and the LDS temple ceremony. Although some argue that Joseph Smith borrowed elements of Freemasonry in developing the temple ceremony, the endowment is more congruous with LDS scriptures (especially the Book of Abraham and the Book of Moses) and ancient ritual than with Freemasonry. Latter-day Saints view the ordinances as a revealed restoration of ancient temple ceremony and only incidentally related to Freemasonry. The two are not antithetical, however, nor do they threaten each other, and neither institution discourages research regarding the ancient origins of their two ceremonies" (Daniel H. Ludlow, ed., *Encyclopedia of Mormonism* [New York: Macmillan, 1992], 2:528). A most productive field of investigation connected with this area lies—as just mentioned—among "ancient ritual." And within that broad category, the most productivity comes in studying the rituals of God's ancient covenant people. A detailed look at this particular topic, however, is not provided in the present volume. Those persons who would like to review ancient rituals may find it worthwhile to examine the contents of Matthew B. Brown, *The Gate of Heaven: Insights on the Doctrines and Symbols of the Temple* (American Fork, UT: Covenant, 1999) and Matthew B. Brown, "Girded about with a Lambskin," *Journal of Book of Mormon Studies*, vol. 6, no. 2, 1997, 124–51.

70. Notice that Bishop Whitney's wife also referred to the temple ordinances as "precious" (*Woman's Exponent,* vol. 7, no. 14, 15 December 1878, 105).

71. Ibid., vol. 20, no. 19, 15 April 1892, 149–50. A comparison between the complete remarks of Newel K. Whitney and

the notes on the first Nauvoo endowment session written by eyewitness Willard Richards (see *HC,* 5:1–2), plus the evident meaning behind some of Whitney's phraseology, confirms that Whitney's words were about the endowment. In addition, the many similarities in theme and language between the two documents suggests that Richards read the Whitney account before composing his reminiscence for the *History of the Church* (the Whitney account was written in a book that was given to the Relief Society by Elder Richards and may have been in his possession when he—in the capacity of Church Historian—wrote *HC,* 5:1–2 in April 1845). Consider these points of congruence—Whitney: "instruction. . . . instructed" / Richards: "instructing"; Whitney: "Priesthood" / Richards: "Priesthood"; Whitney: "certain blessings peculiar to a man of God" / Richards: "washings, anointings, endowments"; Whitney: "God created man. . . . ancient" / Richards: "the Ancient of Days"; Whitney: "the rule given for practice. . . . the law of the Lord" / Richards: "all those plans and principles"; Whitney: "we must lose sight of vain things" / Richards: "the spiritual minded"; Whitney: "blessings . . . of which woman partook" / Richards: "made known to these men . . . will be made known to all the Saints"; Whitney: "fully" / Richards: "fullness"; Whitney: "as soon as our hearts are prepared to receive" / Richards: "so soon as they are prepared to receive"; Whitney: "to bestow" / Richards: "to communicate"; Whitney: "err in judgment many times. . . . failings. . . . strayed" / Richards: "the weakest of the Saints"; Whitney: "humility" / Richards: "meekness"; Whitney: "faithful" / Richards: "faith"; Whitney: "persevere"/ Richards: "perseverance"; Whitney: "assure" / Richards: "assuredly"; Whitney: "Man will not choose, but God will say" / Richards: "governed by the principle of revelation."

72. See *HC,* 5:44–45.

73. See ibid., 5:409.

74. See George D. Smith, ed., *An Intimate Chronicle: The*

Journals of William Clayton (Salt Lake City: Signature Books and Smith Research Associates, 1995), 202, 204.

75. *BYUS,* vol. 19, no. 2, Winter 1979, 145 n. 26.

76. See *HC,* 5:44–45.

77. *T&S,* vol. 6, no. 13, 15 July 1845, 971.

78. See *HC,* 5:409.

79. See Smith, ed., *An Intimate Chronicle: The Journals of William Clayton,* 203–204.

80. See *HC,* 5:44–45.

81. See ibid., 5:409.

82. *T&S,* vol. 5, no. 14, 1 August 1844, 596.

83. See *BYUS,* vol. 19, no. 1, Fall 1978, 86 n. 30.

84. See *T&S,* vol. 3, no. 14, 16 May 1842, 798; ibid., vol. 3, no. 16, 15 June 1842, 830; ibid., vol. 3, no. 17, 1 July 1842, 846.

85. See *HC,* 5:406.

86. See ibid., 5:409.

87. See ibid.; *BYUS,* vol. 19, no. 1, Fall 1978, 86 n. 30.

88. See *T&S,* vol. 4, no. 18, 1 August 1843, 287.

89. See *HC,* 5:44–45.

90. *T&S,* vol. 6, no. 1, 15 January 1845, 781.

91. Ibid., vol. 6, no. 2, 1 February 1845, 799.

92. See Smith, ed., *An Intimate Chronicle: The Journals of William Clayton,* 202.

93. See *HC,* 5:44–45.

94. See ibid., 5:409.

95. See Smith, ed., *An Intimate Chronicle: The Journals of William Clayton,* 202–204.

CHAPTER 7

History, Theory, and Myth

There is no shortage of musing, speculation, and debate when it comes to the subject of Joseph Smith and Freemasonry. Some of the ideas that are advocated—which can be found circulating among critics, bystanders, and Saints alike—are historically grounded, while others venture far into the field of the mythical and the ludicrous. Many of them range somewhere in between. Some of these notions are relatively easy to analyze while others are multifaceted and call for more rigorous examination. But in each case, it is important to carefully scrutinize them so that the past comes more sharply into focus and a more accurate understanding of Church history becomes manifest.

This chapter addresses fifteen of the more commonly championed ideas about the relationship between Mormonism and Masonry and will hopefully help the student of the Restoration to better discern what counts as history and what constitutes theory and myth.

1. There was no contemplated change between the Kirtland and Nauvoo Temple ordinances until after Joseph Smith joined the Masonic fraternity.

A secondhand summary of remarks made by Hyrum Smith on 7 April 1842 is typically used in the attempt to support this viewpoint. The notes of Hyrum's address on that day read as follows:

> Pres[ident] Hyrum Smith spoke concerning the Elders who went forth to preach from Kirtland, [Ohio] and were afterwards called in for the washing and anointing at the dedication of the

House [of the Lord], and those who go now will be called in also, when this Temple is about to be dedicated, and will then be endowed to go forth with mighty power having the same anointing, that all may go forth and have the same power, the first [quorum], second, and so on, of the seventies and all those formerly ordained. This will be an important and beneficial mission, and not many years until those now sent will be called in again.[1]

Since Hyrum is represented here as saying that the Nauvoo and Kirtland Temple anointing would be the "same," some people have drawn the conclusion that by 7 April 1842 there was no plan to have a different type of endowment from the one experienced in Kirtland. There are three things wrong with this perspective, however. First, the context of the secondhand statement is that the anointing in the Nauvoo Temple would endow elders with the same "power" that was bestowed upon the elders who were anointed in the Kirtland Temple. Second, Hyrum Smith knew long before he made the above statement that the practices of the Nauvoo Temple would be in advance of those experienced in the Kirtland sanctuary. In September 1840, he participated in the issuance of a First Presidency letter wherein the Nauvoo Temple's construction was announced, and the Presidency declared their disposition to establish the Priesthood in its fullness.[2] Hyrum was named in the Nauvoo Temple revelation now known as D&C 124, which was given on 19 January 1841. The Lord spoke in that revelation of restoring the fullness of the priesthood, He listed several activities that would go beyond what was practiced in the Kirtland Temple, and He instructed the Prophet to give Hyrum certain temple-related "keys" that had not been given to the endowed elders in Ohio. On 15 June 1841, William W. Phelps stated in print that he had learned from Hyrum Smith that by then "the Lord ha[d] revealed something relative to the fulness of the priesthood, or in other words, new things relating to that sacred order."[3] Third, in his role as Patriarch of the Church, Hyrum Smith informed Heber C. Kimball on 9 March 1842 that he had a right to "the anointing and the end[ow]ment."[4] Elder Kimball had already received the Kirtland Temple anointing on 27 March 1836.[5] If the two anointings were considered to be the same at this point in time (just six days before Joseph Smith became a Freemason), then Elder Kimball would have had no need to receive it again, and Hyrum Smith would have had no need to offer it to him again. Hyrum used the same exact phraseology to refer to the Nauvoo Temple ordinances after he himself had received them. In a patriarchal blessing that he gave on 28 March 1843, he said that the person would receive "the anointing and the endowment."[6]

2. Joseph Smith believed in taking truth from wherever he found it, and so he would not have seen any problem with borrowing from the Freemasons.

There are three main problems with this argument.

A) There is only one instance of the Prophet teaching the "embrace every truth" concept before he bestowed the Nauvoo endowment, and that was in a 22 March 1839 letter to someone who belonged to another church. In this communiqué, Joseph Smith invoked the "embrace every truth" precept as a counterbalance to "the creeds or superstitious notions of men," and he clearly connected "truth" with "the doctrine of the Latter Day Saints." Later in this letter, he also provided the proper context for the "embrace every truth" tenet when, in speaking of the biblical principles and ordinances of the gospel, he asked, "Now where is the man who is authorized to put his finger on the spot and say, 'Thus far shalt thou go and no farther'? There is no man. Therefore, let us receive the whole [i.e., every truth or doctrine of the Bible], or none."[7]

B) Joseph Smith had no need to do any borrowing. The Lord indicated that He would restore the temple rituals of ancient Israel to the Prophet, and He outlined what they were in section 124 of the Doctrine and Covenants. The Prophet was not directed in this revelation to take any action with regard to this issue.

C) About one year and five months before Joseph Smith became a Freemason (5 October 1840), he told the congregants at general conference in Nauvoo, "God will not acknowledge that which He has not called, ordained, and chosen. . . . [T]he ordinances must be kept in the very way God has appointed, otherwise [the] priesthood will prove a cursing instead of a blessing."[8] On 22 January 1843—just a little over eight months after giving the Nauvoo endowment for the first time—the Prophet taught the very same concept, saying, "All the ordinances, systems, and administrations on the earth [are] of no use to the children of men unless they are ordained and authorized of God. For nothing will save a man but a legal administrator, for none others will be acknowledged either by God or angels."[9]

Since the Prophet was teaching near the time of his Masonic initiation that the system of the Masons was "degenerated" and had been "taken from [the] Priesthood,"[10] he certainly would not have viewed its administrations as being ordained and authorized of God, nor efficacious in matters of personal salvation. It should also be emphasized that there is no primary, secondary, or tertiary historical source where Joseph Smith states that he borrowed elements of the Masonic ceremonies.

3. Joseph Smith's intent was to restore Freemasonry to its pure form.

There are no statements (firsthand, secondhand, or otherwise) by the Prophet Joseph Smith indicating that the Nauvoo-era temple ordinances were a form of "purified Masonry." While it is true that in some instances individual Saints referred to the most sacred rituals of their religion as a type of celestial, divine, or true "Masonry" (see claim #12 below), it should be noted that this practice seems to have begun fourteen years after Joseph Smith's death and was instigated by a person who had joined the Masonic lodge many years before he converted to Mormonism—Heber C. Kimball.

The fact that several Masonic—but Mormon-dominated—lodges functioned in the vicinity of Nauvoo at the very same time that temple ordinances were being bestowed upon Mormons forcefully illustrates that the Mormon ordinances were in no way equated with the Masonic rites (i.e., becoming a Mason did not give a person the status of being endowed and vice versa). Furthermore, if Joseph Smith had really intended to "restore" Ancient York Masonry[11] to its pristine state and introduce that untainted version among the Mormons, then his rites should exhibit a pronounced affinity with the stonemasons' rites of old. Yet this is not how things stand. Latter-day Saints who are endowed have absolutely no connection to architects, building laborers, or the science of geometry.

The nature of the Nauvoo Temple ordinances was plainly spelled out by the Lord before they were introduced among the Saints and before Joseph Smith was received into the Masonic fraternity. At the beginning of 1841, the Lord said that Nauvoo Temple activities would be a restoration of rituals once practiced in the Tabernacle built by the prophet Moses and the temple constructed by King Solomon (see D&C 124:37–39). In other words, they would be Hebrew in their basis and content, not Masonic. And this points to another historical fact that needs to be remembered. The Kirtland Temple rituals were a precursor of the Nauvoo Temple ordinances. The Kirtland washing and anointing ceremonies predated Joseph Smith's Masonic membership by six years and four months, and they were specifically, and contemporaneously, linked—by the Saints themselves—to the initiation rites experienced by the priests of ancient Israel.[12]

Again, the basis and content of these ceremonies was Hebrew, not Masonic.

It is important to point out that it would not have been possible for Joseph Smith to restore the speculative Masonry he had personally experienced to its 'pure' form because it simply did not have one. The three fundamental degrees of the speculative Craft were the product of a long evolutionary process that can be traced back in Masonic documents to about AD 1400. The single, and very simple, medieval induction rite for operative stonemasons morphed into two degrees in the 1600s. These dual rites were practiced by operative as well as speculative Masons. In the early 1700s, another change took place, and three degrees for speculative Freemasons began to emerge. And then there was a veritable explosion in the creation of new Masonic degrees. After the Premier Grand Lodge of England was established, "the new Masons gave rein to their imagination, and in the course of one single century they fabricated hundreds . . . of degrees. . . . [and] claimed for all of them a high antiquity."[13] The first three initiation degrees of the speculative Freemasons (including the Royal Arch) were not declared to be the sole representations of "pure ancient Masonry" until the year 1813.[14] Yet some Masonic historians candidly admit that "these three degrees were far from being the original Masonry."[15]

4. *Joseph Smith restored the Nauvoo Temple ordinances through a process of "inspiration."*

A brief statement made by Mormon apostate John C. Bennett is utilized to support the notion of "restoration-through-inspiration." Bennett said in a letter dated 27 June 1842 that Joseph Smith established the temple institution in Nauvoo "by inspiration."[16] Critics claim that this means Joseph Smith viewed the Masonic rites, felt inwardly "inspired" to make modifications to what he saw, and then presented the altered rituals as the endowment. This theory usually does not factor in the possibility of inspiration from an outside, divine source.[17]

The problem with the source used to support this theory is that John C. Bennett published something shortly thereafter that directly refutes it. Bennett stated in a letter scribed on 4 July 1842 that Joseph had said a portion of the temple ceremony was given to him by "revelation."[18] When Bennett wrote about this very same subject in book form later that same year, he specified that Joseph claimed this portion was "revealed" to him by God.[19] There was an external, divine agency involved—not self-contained "inspiration." The very same idea of God revealing a ceremonial element of the temple can be seen in Joseph Smith's testimony given on 15 June 1844. On that occasion he made it known that his seerstone or "Urim and Thummim" was utilized in the acquisition of a particular piece of ceremonial knowledge.[20] The notes the Prophet appended to Facsimile #2 of the book of Abraham make it clear that he learned of temple-related things as he worked with physical texts,[21] and his rendition of part of the Old Testament points to the same conclusion.[22] And one cannot overlook D&C 124:42. In this revelation, the Lord said this with regard to the Nauvoo Temple: "I will show unto my servant Joseph all things pertaining to this house, and the priesthood thereof." A few months after this pronouncement was made, Hyrum Smith affirmed that "the Lord ha[d] revealed something relative to the fulness of the priesthood, or in other words, new things relating to that sacred order."[23] Further evidence of the fulfillment of the D&C 124 promise can be seen in the words of Salt Lake City residents, Elizabeth Whitney, and Eliza Munson, each of whom reported that an angel delivered knowledge of temple-related matters to the Prophet.[24] Elder Parley P. Pratt confirmed this idea, elaborating that "angels and spirits from the eternal worlds" had instructed Joseph Smith in "the mysteries" of the three heavens, including baptism for the dead, anointings, various ordinances, and sealings.[25]

From all of the above sources it can be seen that the Prophet and the Saints who knew him did not hold to the view that the process of temple restoration was based upon one man's inner sense of "inspiration." Instead, they taught that the temple ordinances were restored at the behest of the Lord—through His duly authorized, heavenly representatives and through the power of *divine* revelation.[26]

5. *Joseph Smith employed Masonic terminology long before he joined the Mason's Craft.*

The Prophet's critics believe that they can detect a number of Masonic terms in his writings and vocabulary both before and after he became a Freemason. This, they claim, is proof positive that the development of early Mormonism and its temple rituals are closely tied to the order of Freemasonry. A careful look at the supposed links, however, brings this claim into serious doubt.

The Book of Mormon: Soon after the Book of Mormon was published in 1830, the accusation arose that references in it to things such as a lambskin worn about the loins, a "flaxen cord" placed around the neck, "secret combinations," "secret oaths and covenants," "secret signs," "secret works," a "secret society," and "secret words" all pertained to nineteenth-century Freemasonry—and hence stood as evidence that the volume was not really an ancient text as Joseph Smith claimed. Various LDS writers, on the other hand, have counter-argued that Masonry never did have a proprietary claim on any of these objects, concepts, or phrases. And indeed, these authors have demonstrated that such things can be seen in the ancient world and also in more modern times outside of Masonic circles.[27] One prominent Mormon historian has pointed out that if one takes a close look at the Gadianton Robbers in the Book of Mormon and compares them with what happens in Freemasonry, they will discover a wide disparity. The Gadianton band has no connection with Solomon's Temple, there are no descriptions of "elaborate initiation rituals" or progressive degrees among them, and there are no references—or even allusions—to the main personas found in Masonic history and drama.[28] The one thing that (more than any other) negates the charge that Masonic elements were put into the Book of Mormon text is the testimony of the Three Witnesses. They saw an angel of God appear before them with a tableful of metallic records and historical articles. They watched as the angel turned over the leaves of the golden record whence the Book of Mormon writings were obtained and listened as the voice of the Lord confirmed the accuracy of the translation.[29]

The Book of Moses: Joseph Smith's critics have long maintained that the title "Master Mahan" in the fifth chapter of the book of Moses (vv. 31, 49) is a thinly disguised variation of "Master Mason"—the designation for Freemasonry's third degree of initiation. Footnote *d* for Moses 5:31 in the LDS edition of the book of Moses, however, offers several possible meanings for the word *Mahan* based upon its etymological root. Of the choices that are offered, "destroyer" seems to be a strong candidate. The Hebrew word *māhâ* carries the basic meaning of "wipe out . . . destroy,"[30] and the addition of the letter *n* at the end of the word could make it a noun.[31] Hence, the word *Mahan* could be interpreted to mean "destroyer" (cf. Gen. 4:8). This fits well with Cain's own statement in the Book of Moses after making a pact with Satan: "Truly I am *Mahan,* the *master* of this great secret, that I may murder [or destroy] and get gain" (5:31; emphasis added). Destruction is one of the attributes applied to Satan in Moses 4:6 and also in several New Testament passages (see John 8:44; 1 Cor. 5:5; Heb. 2:14; 1 Pet. 5:8). The title "Mahan" is thus fitting for a follower of the devil. Neither the content nor the context of any of this can rightly be applied to those persons who rise to the rank of a Master Mason in a Freemason's lodge.

Reminiscence: Comments attributed to the Prophet in his diary dated 29 December 1835 (but actually written by his scribe

Warren Parrish) have led some people to conclude that Joseph Smith was using Masonic phraseology at the time. He is represented in this record as saying, "I had liberty in speaking. Some Presbyterians were present, as I afterwards learned, and I expect that some of my sayings set like a garment that was well fitted, as I exposed their abominations in the language of the scriptures, and I pray God that it may be like a nail in a sure place, driven by the master of assemblies."[32] Some people are, curiously, of the opinion that the terms "well fitted," "abominations," and "driven by the master of assemblies" are exclusive to Masons. Aside from "well fitted" (which is applied to a garment, and not to a stone), the terminology in the statement credited to the Prophet can be traced to the King James Bible. In Isaiah 22:23, for instance, the Lord says, "I will fasten him as a nail in a sure place," and in Ecclesiastes 12:11, it is said that the words of the wise are "as nails fastened by the masters of assemblies." It hardly needs to be pointed out that the word *abominations* has a clear biblical background (see 2 Chron. 36:14; Jer. 7:30; Ezek. 7:8; Rev. 17:4–5).

Statement to a Private Group: There is a thirdhand declaration credited to Joseph Smith that calls for some comment because it does include a term employed by the Freemasons. Dimick B. Huntington remembered this thirty-four years after the fact:

> One night after work was over in the [Nauvoo] lodge [and he] was through working old brother [Asahel] Perry, the tiler [or doorkeeper], said, "A brother wishes to enter." "Let him enter" [was the response]: George A. Smith [the Prophet's cousin] was the Master [of the lodge]. Joseph Smith entered [and] strode up and down the lodge saying, "Hallelujah . . . I have done what King Solomon, King Hiram, and Hiram Abiff could not do. I have set up the kingdom no more to be thrown down forever nor never to be given to another people."[33]

The name Hiram Abiff plays a central role in some Masonic initiation work, but its origin and the timing of the Prophet's reported use of it need clarification. Because the beginning portion of the record where the Huntington quote is found talks about the 4 May 1842 endowment session, some people assume that the last portion of the Huntington quote (as reproduced above) is talking about the same time frame. They then errone-ously tie together the first practice of the Nauvoo Temple ordi-nances and the Masonic term supposedly uttered by the Prophet. The reason why the inaugural endowment ceremony and the Hiram Abiff utterance should not be joined together is because Joseph Smith did not set up the prototypical kingdom of God until March 1844.[34] The Hiram Abiff comment, therefore, has no connection to the introduction of the endowment. In fact, it was made long after Joseph Smith became a Freemason, and he mentioned it while inside a Masonic lodge and among a group of Freemasons. Still, it needs to be acknowledged that the name Hiram Abiff was not created by the Masons. It can be found in the translations of the Bible produced by Martin Luther and Miles Coverdale (see 2 Chron. 2:13; 4:16). It should also be noted that the Prophet's message to the men in the lodge in 1844 was not centered on Freemasonry, but rather on the fulfill-ment of biblical prophecy concerning the establishment of God's latter-day kingdom (see Jer. 31:40; Dan. 2:44; Matt. 21:43).

6. *Joseph Smith patterned the Nauvoo Relief Society after Masonic structure and ideology.*

There are a number of arguments that are associated with this premise. Following are seven of the most common ones that try to tie the Relief Society organization to Freemasonry.

(A) *The Nauvoo Relief Society was formed in the same room where the Freemasons held their meetings.*

While this statement is accurate, it is likewise true that the upper room of Joseph Smith's redbrick mercantile store was one of the few enclosed spaces in Nauvoo in early 1842 that had enough room for large assemblies of people. And it was used for many different purposes—not just for the gatherings of the Relief Society and the Masons. It functioned as Church headquarters,[35] played host to convocations of the city council, the city court, political conventions, and also functioned as a welcoming hall for people who had just immigrated to the city.[36] School classes and debates were held there.[37] It was used as a drama theater[38] and a lecture hall.[39] It was also a storage area for the redbrick store's reserve merchandise.[40] The Temple Committee, the Nauvoo House Committee, and members of the Nauvoo Legion all met there.[41] The *History of the Church* makes it clear that the Freemasons only met in the upper room of the redbrick store because they did not have anywhere else to go.[42] The Relief Society also met outdoors on occasion[43] but since they never engaged in any type of Masonic activity, it did not matter that they were conducting their business out-of-doors.

(B) *The Nauvoo Relief Society was formed on the day after Joseph Smith became a Freemason.*

This statement is also accurate. But the historical record indicates that the Prophet had stated his desire to organize the Relief Society prior to his becoming a Freemason. And he also said—before his Masonic induction took place—that the women of Nauvoo were going to be organized in accordance with the pattern set forth in the priesthood quorums[44] (which had previously been established by the Lord in several of His revelations).

(C) *A Masonic prayer was written at the beginning of the record book of the Nauvoo Relief Society and is connected with the first meeting of the association held on 17 March 1842.*

The prayer on the first page of the Nauvoo Relief Society minute book is, indeed, Masonic in character. The text of this prayer is as follows: "O, Lord! help our widows, and fatherless children! So mote it be. Amen. With the sword, and the word

of truth, defend thou them. So mote it be. Amen."[45] While
the phrase "So mote it be" certainly marks this as a distinctly
Masonic form of prayer, it should also be noted that the core
themes of this appeal are found right in the Bible. The "fatherless
and widows" are mentioned in such places as James 1:27, Psalms
68:5, Jeremiah 49:11, and Lamentations 5:3. The defense of the
poor and fatherless is located in Psalms 82:3, while the phrase
"word of truth" can be seen in such scriptures as Psalms 119:43,
2 Corinthians 6:7, and 2 Timothy 2:15.

The questions that need to be answered with regard to this
piece of historical information include, "When was it written
on the first page of the Relief Society ledger?" "Who determined
that it would be recorded there?" and "What was the motivation
for recording it?" An explanatory note that accompanied the
prayer helps to answer these questions. It said: "The following
appropriate frontispiece was found lying on an open Bible, in the
room appropriated for the Society; at its first meeting. Written
on a scrap." Since the piece of paper with the prayer was placed
on top of an open Bible, odds are that the prayer was utilized
during the Prophet's Masonic initiation the previous day (the
Masons always have an open Bible or other volume of sacred
law in their lodge room while they conduct business). Notice,
however, that the explanatory note is written in past tense. It
should further be stated that the note precedes the prayer in
order of placement on the page where it is inscribed. Both of
these facts tend to indicate that the prayer was not copied into
the Relief Society record at the inaugural women's meeting in
1842. The time of its recording is otherwise unknown. Another
thing that is significant about the note is that it specifies that the
prayer was "found" by an unidentified person—not that it was
presented to the women as a whole by any Church authority as
part of the establishment of their society. The note is also important because it indicates exactly why somebody decided to place
a transcription of the prayer in the official record book: they

thought its contents were "appropriate" to the congregation. The sentiments contained in the prayer were not new to the Saints, however. The idea of caring for widows and the fatherless was advocated in the Church's official newspapers during the early 1830s.[46] In 1840, this concept was being tied, by the Mormons, to consecration of oneself to the Lord,[47] and in 1841, it was being encouraged through an epistle written by the Quorum of the Twelve Apostles.[48]

(D) *At the first meetings of the Relief Society (March 17th and 30th, 1842), Joseph Smith used Masonic terminology with relation to the group.*

"Constitution" and "bylaws." These terms were in prominent use among Freemasons, but they were not exclusively Masonic, nor were they introduced to the woman's group by Joseph Smith. Sarah Kimball testified that it was the women themselves who on 4 March 1842 (before the introduction of Freemasonry into Nauvoo) wrote up their own constitution and bylaws for a ladies society. These items were presented to the Prophet before the Nauvoo Lodge was formed, and he said at the time that he would organize the women with something better than a written constitution.[49] Such terms were not new to the Latter-day Saints in 1842. Constitutions and bylaws had been set up for the Kirtland Safety Society in 1837 and the Nauvoo Agricultural and Manufacturing Association in 1841.[50]

"Grow up by degrees." Some commentators have tried to make this phrase out to be Masonic, since the three fundamental levels of Freemasonry are commonly referred to as "degrees." But a close look at the Relief Society minute book reveals that the context of Joseph's remark was completely different. He said that the sisters "were going too fast—that the society should grow up by degrees; should commence with a few individuals."[51] Hence, his concern was numerically based. And it must be remembered that there were no "degrees" of membership in the Relief Society.

"A close examination of every candidate." While it is true that the rules of Masonry called for the determination of a person's character before they were admitted to initiation, it is likewise true that the Mormons were engaging in such a practice long before the Nauvoo Lodge was formed. The "due examination" of "candidates" for baptism was reported in the LDS Church's newspaper[52] back in 1836, and "due examination" before ordination to office was noted the same year.[53]

"Electing . . . to . . . office" and "elect lady." The Freemasons did elect their officers, but the Latter-day Saints did also before the Nauvoo Lodge was founded. Again, the Kirtland Safety Society in 1837 and the Nauvoo Agricultural and Manufacturing Association of 1841 are examples.[54] Some commentators have asserted that there was a connection between the Prophet's use of the phrase "elect lady" and the French Rite of Adoption, which was a pseudo-Masonic women's organization. Yet on the very same day when Joseph Smith applied this title to his wife, he recited a revelation given in 1830 wherein the Lord gave her the identical designation.[55]

(E) *The Nauvoo Relief Society had offices that were also part of a Masonic Lodge.*

The officers of an American Masonic Lodge in the nineteenth century included a Worshipful Master, Senior Warden, Junior Warden, Senior Deacon, Junior Deacon, Secretary, Treasurer, and Tiler. The officers of the Relief Society, on the other hand, were designated by the Prophet Joseph Smith as a "Presidency," consisting of a "presiding officer" or "President" or "Chairman" and "two counselors."[56] Other officers of the women's group included a treasurer and a secretary,[57] but these offices were not uniquely Masonic. Indeed, the Latter-day Saints had elected a treasurer and secretary for the Kirtland Safety Society[58] at the beginning of 1837 and the same for the Nauvoo Agricultural and Manufacturing Association[59] in the first quarter of 1841.

(F) *LDS Church leaders referred to Relief Society members as "Masons" in an epistle that was read at a meeting on 30 March 1842.*

This epistle was recorded in the Relief Society record book,[60] and the signatories included Joseph Smith, Brigham Young, Heber C. Kimball, Willard Richards, Hyrum Smith, and Vinson Knight. Only three of these six men were Freemasons at the time, but it should be noted that Joseph Smith had only become a Mason two weeks before. The part of this epistle that is of interest states,

> We do not mention [certain person's] names [in this epistle], not knowing but what there may be some among you who are not sufficiently skilled in Masonry as to keep a secret. . . . Let this epistle be had as a private matter in your Society, and then we shall learn whether you are good Masons.

The comparison of the women of the Relief Society to Masons was clearly figurative, not to be taken in a literal way. The presiding brethren wanted the women to assimilate an attribute that was prominently advocated in the Freemason's lodge, but they did not ascribe any other meaning to it. Joseph Smith gave a clue as to why he and the others focused on the principle of secrecy when he told the Relief Society sisters on 28 April 1842 that he was going to deliver to them certain temple-related "keys,"[61] and then on 1 May 1842, he taught that these very same keys could only be revealed inside of the Nauvoo Temple.[62] Then he reiterated on 15 October 1843 that "the secret of Masonry is to keep a secret."[63]

(G) *Joseph Smith's intent was to establish the Relief Society as a women's Masonic lodge.*

If this were true, then there should have been some initiatic correspondence between the Relief Society and the Freemasons. But this simply was not the case. There was no initiation ceremony whereby a woman in Nauvoo joined the ranks of the

Relief Society. In fact, just the opposite was true. Early Church
leaders such as Joseph Smith and Newel K. Whitney said that
the Relief Society was to be organized "after the pattern of the
Priesthood"[64] so as to *prepare* them to receive the initiation
ordinances of the Nauvoo Temple.[65] In other words, the Relief
Society was to function partly as a way station for women before
they became part of "a kingdom of priestesses."[66]

7. *There were several Masonic patterns incorporated into the Kirtland Temple.*

This claim focuses on the cornerstone ceremonies, architectural motifs, and seating arrangements of the building.

The origin of the Latter-day Saint cornerstone ordinances
can be found in a revelation dated 6 May 1833. In this communication from heaven, Jesus Christ said this with regard to the
Kirtland Temple: "It shall be dedicated unto the Lord from the
foundation thereof, according to the order of the priesthood,
according to the pattern which shall be given unto you hereafter" (D&C 94:6). There were marked dissimilarities between
the Mormon and the Masonic cornerstone ceremonies that
need to be acknowledged. The Masons dedicated one stone;
the Mormons dedicated four stones. The Masons utilized corn,
wine, and oil during their rite; the Mormons used no such
materials. The Masons used an architectural implement to
symbolically try the trueness of the cornerstone; the Mormons
did not do any corresponding act. The Masonic ceremony could
be carried out with only a handful of people participating; the
Mormon ceremony required a large, set number of priesthood
holders.[67]

There is documentary evidence that the pattern of the
Kirtland Temple did not come from an earthly source. In a
revelation dated 1 June 1833, the Lord said, "Let the house be
built, not after the manner of the world, for I give not unto
you that ye shall live after the manner of the world. Therefore,

let it be built after the manner which I shall show unto three of you, whom ye shall appoint and ordain unto this power" (D&C 95:13–14). Witnesses heard Frederick G. Williams testify that he, Sidney Rigdon, and Joseph Smith were shown a vision of the exterior and interior of the Kirtland Temple, and it was built "like the pattern precisely," even "to a minutia [sic]."[68] Several early nineteenth-century newspapers verify that the Mormons were teaching that this was how the plan of the temple was conceived. Following are three examples from the year 1836.

• "The pattern . . . was given by direct revelation from heaven, and given to three individuals separately, so that there could be no doubt on the subject."[69]

• "It is of no earthly order of architecture, but the Prophet says is exactly according to the pattern showed him, though it is by no means equal to that in splendor from the want of means."[70]

• "The plan [of the Kirtland Temple], even to the minutiae, they say was revealed, by God, to the Prophet Smith" and two other people.[71]

In a letter about the Kirtland Temple's counterpart in Missouri, dated 25 June 1833, the First Presidency of the LDS Church (who were the persons shown the aforementioned vision) described several architectural features of the building, including an arched ceiling, Gothic doors and windows with Venetian blinds, a belfry, slip pews, choir seats, a fanlight, painted shingles, tiered pulpit stands or coves for the high (west) and lesser (east) priesthoods, curtains to divide the main chamber into four sections, and also veils to divide the pulpit stands into private areas.[72] None of these features are considered to be a Masonic invention or a distinctive architectural style of speculative Masonry. A check of some of the popular architectural manuals of the day reveals that those manuals were the source of several of the decorative motifs associated with the Kirtland Temple—not the Freemasons.[73]

The final point to be considered is the priesthood pulpits. Elder Orson Pratt confirmed that God

> revealed the pattern according to which that house should be built, pointing out the various courts and apartments, telling the size of the house, *the order of the pulpits,* and in fact everything pertaining to it was clearly pointed out by revelation. God gave a vision of these things, not only to Joseph, but to several others, and they were strictly commanded to build according to the pattern revealed from the heavens.[74]

While it is true, in a general sense, that officiators in the Kirtland Temple and Masonic lodges were seated in the east and the west, there were significant differences between the two arrangements. For instance, there were twenty-four Mormons but only seven Masons. In the temple, there were twelve people stationed in both the east and the west while the Masons placed four in the east, two in the west, and one in the south. The Mormon individuals were priesthood holders of the Melchizedek and Aaronic orders while the Masons were supervisors and administrators. The highest Mormon authority sat on the west side of the Kirtland Temple while the highest Masonic authority always sat in the east. The Mormon pulpits rose in four tiers on both the east and the west ends of the room while the Masons raised the highest eastern officiator (only) on three steps, the highest western officiator (only) on two steps, and the sole southern officiator on two steps. The only corresponding office between the two sets of dignitaries was that of deacon. In the Kirtland Temple, the three-man presidency over the deacons quorum sat together on the east side while in the lodge, the Senior Deacon sat in the east, but the Junior Deacon sat in the west. The Masons had a Senior and Junior Warden, a Secretary, a Treasurer, and a Worshipful Master sitting in their assigned places. The Mormons had no such officers sitting in their pulpits.

The bottom tiers of the Mormon pulpits, on both sides, were equipped with sacrament tables. The sacrament was not served during the procedures of the lodge. Cloth partitions were utilized in the various compartments of the Mormon pulpits to facilitate privacy in prayer. No partitions of this sort were used when Masonic initiates became Entered Apprentices, Fellow Crafts, or Master Masons. Another difference in the seats of the two institutions is that the Mormon pulpits were considered to have a special sanctity: they were "dedicated . . . and consecrated" by priesthood authority prior to the dedication of the entire temple.[75] This was not the case with the Masonic chairs. Lastly, it should be noted that the twenty-four seats for priesthood holders in the Kirtland Temple mirror the twenty-four seats in the heavenly temple where kings and priests are seated (see Rev. 4:4; 5:8–10).

8. *The celestial room of the Nauvoo Temple was decorated with Masonic emblems.*

This claim rests on the fact that there were two free-standing, spherical atlases (one of the heavens and one of the earth) on a small table near the eastern window of the celestial room in the Nauvoo Temple.[76] These were not the only maps in that compartment of the building, however. According to the contemporary record of William Clayton, there was "a large map of the world hang[ing] on the north side wall, and three maps of the United States and a plot [or map] of the city of Nauvoo hang[ing] on the west partition. On the south wall [hung] another large map of the United States."[77] Altogether, there were eight maps displayed in the celestial room of the Nauvoo Temple, but only two of them were depicted on globes. The spherical maps of the continents and the stars may, therefore, have been nothing more than decorations to beautify the most meaningful area of the temple.[78]

Some of the speculative Freemasons of the nineteenth century incorporated globular maps of the heavens and the earth into the furniture of their lodges and in various iconographical formats, having adopted the idea partly from illustrated Bibles of AD 1560 and later[79] and possibly from artworks such as Raphael Santi's 1510 painting called *The School of Athens*. This Renaissance depiction—which is housed in the Vatican—shows men holding spherical maps of both the heavens and the earth (right next to Euclid, who seems to be sketching out a geometric figure with a pair of compasses).

There is no indication in the source document that the globes in the Nauvoo Temple were borrowed from a Masonic Lodge or were considered to represent any specific Masonic ideology. Indeed, the circular atlases in the celestial room may well have come from the University of the City of Nauvoo, where Apostle Orson Pratt was teaching courses on astronomy and mensuration[80] or the art of measurement[81]—which could include the exercise of determining the surface of a twenty-four-inch globe or the entire spherical earth.[82] In connection with all of this, it is interesting to note that during some down time in the Nauvoo Temple on 27 December 1845, Elder Orson Pratt busied himself by making "astronomical calculations."[83]

9. *The symbols on the exterior of the Nauvoo and Salt Lake temples are Masonic.*

Some people see the sun, moon, and stars on the exterior of the Nauvoo Temple and conclude that since Joseph Smith became a Freemason during the same general time period as when the temple was being built—and the speculative Masons sometimes employed the sun, moon, and stars in their iconography—the Prophet must have borrowed these emblems from Freemasonry.

There are two major problems with this viewpoint. The first problem is that the Mormons had incorporated these emblems into their culture long before Masonry was introduced into Nauvoo. Joseph Smith created many documents (of a scriptural nature) that included sun, moon, and stars imagery prior to his induction into the Masonic fraternity. These texts stretched from the late 1820s through the end of the 1830s.[84] Additionally, Joseph Smith is known to have used sun, moon, and stars imagery in historical writings[85] and also as he spoke during the same time frame.[86] Latter-day Saints, in general, were regularly exposed to sun, moon, and stars images. They sang about them in hymns[87] and read about them in Church periodicals such as the *Evening and Morning Star*, the *Messenger and Advocate*, the *Elders' Journal*, the *Times and Seasons*, and the *Millennial Star*. Articles in these newspapers connected the sun, moon, and stars with signs of the impending Millennium, degrees of post-resurrection glory, a dream had by Joseph of Egypt, the Creation, order in the universe, sources of light, and the Lord's bride or true Church of Jesus Christ.

This last mentioned item calls for special attention because of its connection to the main symbols on the outside of the Nauvoo Temple. Wandle Mace was one of the temple foremen who were in charge of erecting the structure, and he plainly stated that the sun, moon, and stars of the exterior were meant to portray something that is described in Revelation 12:1. That scripture describes a woman standing on the moon who is clothed with the sun and has a crown of stars upon her head. The Nauvoo Temple emblems, said Brother Mace, followed this same pattern and were thus "a representation of the Church, the Bride, the Lamb's wife"[88] (cf. Rev. 19:6–9). Back in 1832, Joseph Smith had identified the woman who stood on the moon as "the church of God" (JST, Rev. 12:7). In 1835, an article in the *Messenger and Advocate* called the woman standing on the moon "the church of Christ as established by the apostles, adorned with the glory and power of God . . . or [the] perfect church, as sanctioned by God."[89] It is interesting to note that starting in May 1841 and going through February 1842, Hyrum Smith (a long-standing Freemason) incorporated the Revelation 12:1 images into some of the patriarchal blessings that he gave to women.[90]

The second problem with the theory of borrowing the sun, moon, and stars motifs from the Masons is that Joseph Smith claimed that the architectural order of the Nauvoo Temple was given to him through a divine source. In a revelation on the Nauvoo Temple dated 19 January 1841, the Lord stated, "I will show unto my servant Joseph all things pertaining to this house" (D&C 124:42). A non-Mormon who attended the cornerstone laying ceremonies for this temple on 6 April 1841 reported his understanding that "the dimensions, architecture, arrangement, and devotions" of the temple had all been revealed to the Church President "with no less minuteness than were those of the ancient Jewish sanctuary."[91] In January 1843, a non-Mormon wrote in a letter from Nauvoo that the Prophet was professing that the temple's style of architecture had been given to him "by divine revelation."[92] On 5 February 1844, the Prophet reiterated to the temple architect that he had "seen in vision the splendid appearance of that building" and insisted that it be erected according to the "pattern" he had been shown.[93] That this pattern included decorative emblems can be seen in the fact that in the spring of 1844, President Smith was asked by a temple workman with regard to one of the sunstones he was carving, "Is this like the face you saw in vision?" To which the reply was, "Very near it."[94]

Other symbols that are known to have decorated the outside of the Nauvoo Temple included stylized clouds, hands holding trumpets, a plaque that said "Holiness to the Lord,"[95] and a supine angel in priestly robes who held a trumpet and a Book of Mormon.[96] The cloud, trumpet, and sacral clothing are all items associated with the temples of ancient Israel.[97] Symbols that are found on architectural drawings of the Nauvoo Temple but which have never been verified as actually being incorporated into the building include the all-seeing eye of God[98] and a compass and square touching at their apexes.[99] The all-seeing eye was an emblem that decorated Nauvoo's Masonic lodge (built in 1844),[100] but the Latter-day Saints had laid claim to that symbol from the earliest days of the Restoration.[101] The compass and square seem, to some individuals, to be an obvious appropriation of Masonic emblems. Yet their configuration in the Nauvoo Temple architectural drawing where they are displayed is not typically Masonic, and in conference minutes from Alabama printed in the Church's newspaper in 1845 a comparison was made between these same implements and the Bible and the Doctrine and Covenants.[102] This happens to be the general context of their placement in the architectural plans of the temple—they are situated right next to the Book of Mormon held by the angel. One must also not forget that Parley P. Pratt reported in his autobiography that in the year 1830 he was shown shapes that corresponded to these particular instruments in a heavenly vision, and they were not displayed to him in Masonic fashion either.[103] It should further be noted that the compass and square are biblical symbols in the sense that they were mentioned in the 1599 Geneva Bible in a footnote for 1 Corinthians chapter 3 verse 3.[104]

It should be added that several people who lived in Nauvoo and who visited the city did not feel that the temple's exterior symbols were Masonic in character. Rather, they said things such as, "The order of architecture was unlike anything in existence; it was purely original";[105] "The style of architecture is unlike any other upon earth";[106] "Nothing can be more original in architecture";[107] "The 'order' of the temple is purely original, not being fashioned after any other order in existence."[108]

The symbols that embellish the outside of the Salt Lake Temple were simply an expanded and modified version of the emblems that adorned the temple in Nauvoo. Earthstones were added to the bottom of the pilasters, the moon was shown transitioning through all of its phases, the clouds (with planned, but never executed, trumpets) were moved to the east end of the building, and the stars were placed on the keystones of the windows and doors. The Big Dipper was added to the west central tower, and acanthus buds topped small finials on all of the towers. Instead of one angelic weathervane, the Salt Lake sanctuary was originally to have two, but this idea was abandoned in favor of a single, large angel on the east center spire. It was at first contemplated that the planet Saturn would be shown among a field of stars near the roofline of the temple and that the earthstones would display the continents, but neither plan was carried out. Some of the architectural drawings for the Salt Lake Temple show that the compass and square were going to be shown next to the oval windows, but this was another feature that never came to fruition.[109] The clasped hands on the Salt Lake Temple are sometimes identified by observers as a symbol of the Masons, but this, again, was an image that had been employed by the Latter-day Saints from very early times.[110] Also, it must be pointed out that the architect of the Salt Lake Temple informed the third President of the LDS Church, in writing, that none of the symbols on the building's exterior were meant to be Masonic.[111]

10. *A temple worker in 1845 used Masonic terminology in referring to the Nauvoo Temple ceremony.*

The information that is used to draw this conclusion comes from John D. Lee's journal (which is kept in the LDS Church's historical records repository) in an entry dated 16 December 1845. It reads as follows:

> About 4 o'clock in the morning I entered the porch in the lower court where I met the porter who admitted me through the door which led to the foot, or nearly so, of a great flight of stairs which, by ascending, led me to the door of the outer court [of the attic story] which I found tiled within by an officer. I, having the proper implements of that degree, gained admittance through

the outer and inner courts which opened and led to the sacred departments [i.e., the endowment rooms]. . . . Having entered, I found myself alone with the Tiler that kept the inner courts [and I/ we] set about and soon got fires up in the different rooms and setting things in order for the day.

Even though the word *degree* is used as a Masonic term, John D. Lee did not utilize it in the typical Masonic way for referring to an initiatic rank or status. Instead, it appears that Lee was applying the word *degree* to "a distinct portion of space"[112]—the attic story where he was assigned to perform certain duties. The terms *porch* and *great flight of stairs* have Masonic analogs also, but in Lee's statement they are references to architectural features of the Nauvoo Temple, not a Masonic lodge.

There is no ambiguity about the terms "Tiler" (a guard at the door of a Mason's lodge) and "tiled"—they are definitely Masonic. Notice, however, that John also used the usual term "porter" to identify a doorway guard—a term which is not considered to be Masonic. It may be that the word *Tiler* was used by Lee simply because he was a fairly new Freemason,[113] and he was applying a term that was used in the lodge environment to refer to the exact same type of activity he encountered at the top of the stairs—the guarding of an entryway.

John D. Lee was one of many volunteers who wanted to help with the operational work of the Nauvoo Temple. He was assigned by Brigham Young on 15 December 1845 (only one day before he made his Tiler comments) to act as a clerk and also "to attend to fires in the rooms and upper apartment, etc.," meaning the ordinance areas in the attic.[114] The William Clayton journal speaks of "door keepers" who were assigned to their posts in the Nauvoo Temple both before and after Lee made his comments about the Tiler.[115] Clayton never used the term "Tiler" to refer to the doorkeepers. The temple doorkeeper was not a new position among the Latter-day Saints, either.

Doorkeepers were assigned to stand at the entryways of the Kirtland Temple nine years earlier,[116] and in the *History of the Church,* the entry guards for the Nauvoo Temple were called "doorkeepers."[117]

It is clear that John D. Lee's references had nothing at all to do with the temple ordinances themselves because he was inside the sanctuary at four o'clock in the morning, and no rituals were being performed at that time. In light of the full quotation from Lee's journal, it can be surmised that the "implements" that gained him admittance through "the door of the outer court" may have simply been pieces of firewood.

11. *Early LDS Church leaders believed the mythological stories about the Freemasons descending from King Solomon's Temple.*

One of the quotations from Brigham Young that is used to substantiate this statement runs as follows: "Who was the founder of Freemasonry? They can go back as far as Solomon, and there they stop. There is the king who established this high and holy order."[118] Notice in this quote that President Young was simply repeating what the Masons themselves had claimed with regard to their historical background. Notice also that he was not giving a treatise on the origins of the Freemasons. Nevertheless, he said in the same statement where this information is found that the Freemasons "were Christians originally." The only reason he brought up King Solomon was because the Masons claimed him as their founder, even though the Bible reported that he was a practitioner of polygamy. Brigham Young was complaining in this discourse that the Masons refused Mormons "membership in their lodge, because they were polygamists."

Another quote from Brigham Young on this subject reads as follows:

> It is true that Solomon built a temple for the purpose of giving endowments but from what

we can learn of the history of that time they gave very few, if any, endowments. And one of the high priests [i.e., Hiram Abiff] was murdered by wicked and corrupt men, who had already begun to apostatize, because he would not reveal those things appertaining to the Priesthood that were forbidden him to reveal until he came to the proper place.[119]

This statement is a mixture of a Masonic storyline and LDS concepts. Still, President Young was simply repeating what the Freemasons had taught him during his own initiation in Nauvoo, Illinois, in 1842. He evidently trusted that they had told him the truth.

Heber C. Kimball taught that "the Masonry of today is received from the apostasy which took place in the days of Solomon, and David."[120] It appears from this statement that Brother Kimball believed that there was a real connection between the Craft and the celebrated sovereigns of the Bible. He would have been introduced to this idea in 1823 when he joined the lodge in Victor, New York. His pronouncement indicates that he trusted the veracity of what his Masonic brethren had told him.

It is sometimes argued by critics that since Brigham Young and Heber C. Kimball were "prophets, seers, and revelators," they should have known the truth about the mythological connection between Freemasonry and King Solomon's Temple. But there is no documented evidence that either of these Church leaders ever requested the Lord to tell them about the origins of this fraternal and charitable organization. And they had little reason to approach the Lord on such a matter since—as Elder Kimball wrote in a letter in 1842—Joseph Smith had already taught them the basics about the origin of Freemasonry.[121]

Many modern Freemasons understand that in America in the early 1800s there was a "general (and false) assumption

that Freemasonry never changed" and because "rumor, speculation, theory, and fact were all given equal credence by some
writers," the conclusion was drawn that the common practices
and customs of Masonry "must have been followed by King
Solomon." It was not until 1884 in London, England, that
"a group of serious students of Freemasonry came together to
form the first lodge devoted to properly documented Masonic
history." Thus, during the lifetimes of Brigham Young and
Heber C. Kimball, the "romantic school" of Masonic history
prevailed. The "authentic school" approach did not start taking
shape until after they had both died.[122]

12. *Various nineteenth- and early twentieth-century Mormons referred to the temple ordinances as "Masonry."*

Apparently the first statement of this nature can be traced no
farther back than 9 November 1858 and comes from a person
who joined the Masonic fraternity long before he converted to
Mormonism. On that day, Heber C. Kimball said, "We have the
true Masonry. The [Free] Masonry of today. . . . [has] now and
then a thing that is correct, but we [i.e., the Mormons] have the
real thing."[123]

Elder Franklin D. Richards said something very similar on
4 April 1899, and he also pointed to the reason why the LDS
ordinances are considered to be the true version of the rites
under question. He said, "Joseph [Smith] enquired of the Lord
concerning [the keys that Masonry admitted were lost] and
He revealed to the Prophet true Masonry, as we have it in our
temples."[124] This perspective helps to clarify why Brigham Young
reportedly delighted in calling the temple rituals "Celestial
Masonry"[125] and why Heber C. Kimball's daughter (Helen Marr
Whitney) would call God the "Great Master Mason."[126] One
dissident from the LDS Church wrote in 1870 that "it is taught
[by Mormons] that there is a sort of divine Masonry among the
angels who hold the Priesthood."[127] And as late as 8 January

1902, Apostle Matthias F. Cowley "spoke of Freemasonry as being a counterfeit of the true Masonry of the Latter-day Saints."[128]

None of these statements is meant to imply that the LDS temple ordinances are a species of speculative Freemasonry. They are, rather, ways of expressing the idea that there is a divine or heavenly prototype, and the LDS version of the ordinances is derived from the heavenly source—and thus constitutes the true version.

13. *A late nineteenth-century Mormon historian stated in print that "Mormonism is Masonic."*

The historian who made this remark was Edward W. Tullidge,[129] and the publication where his comment appeared was called *The Women of Mormondom*.[130] Even though Edward was an on-again-off-again member of the LDS Church, and sometimes a friendly historian and commentator on things Mormon, he never held the position of historian for The Church of Jesus Christ of Latter-day Saints. After he had joined himself with the Reorganized sect in 1879, he became a historian for that ecclesiastical organization.[131]

It needs to be pointed out that Tullidge's *Women of Mormondom* contains several strange references both to Freemasonry and to Mormonism. For example, he speaks of "the celestial Masonry of Womanhood" (even though nineteenth-century women were not allowed to become regular Freemasons),[132] "the Masonic question" of Job 38:4 in the Bible,[133] "a glorious Masonic scheme among the Gods,"[134] and a woman Mormon temple worker being "a Mason, of the Hebraic order."[135] In a book written the following year, which was brought into disrepute by LDS Church leader John Taylor,[136] Tullidge said that "the Masonic Church on earth ought to be in constant communion with the Masonic Church in the heavens."[137] And more than a decade later, Tullidge referred to "the Masonic drama of the fall of man"[138] and claimed that "to the Mormons the Logan Temple is a grand Masonic fabric" which is looked upon as "the Masonic embodiment" of polygamic theocracy.[139] Edward Tullidge's personal views about Masons and Mormons should certainly not be considered to represent the official—much less normative—stance of the Church founded through the Prophet Joseph Smith.

14. The First Presidency of the LDS Church admitted in 1911 that Mormon temple rituals include "Masonic characters."

On 4 November 1911, the *Deseret News* reprinted an article wherein the First Presidency of the LDS Church—then consisting of Joseph F. Smith, Anthon H. Lund, and John Henry Smith—gave an account of Church history. This article was subsequently included in the book entitled *Messages of the First Presidency of The Church of Jesus Christ of Latter-day Saints*. One of the sentences in this article says, "Because of their Masonic characters the ceremonies of the temple are sacred and not for the public."[140] Some individuals see this as proof that the highest governing body of the Mormon Church admitted that the temple endowment incorporated "Masonic characters" or elements.

The article printed in the *Deseret News,* however, was not the original. This article had previously been published in the *Oakland Tribune* and had been explicitly created for a non-LDS audience (which may explain its reference to Masonry). A check of the *Tribune*'s rendition of this publicity piece indicates that the letter *s* was inadvertently added to the word *character* when the reprint occurred in the *Deseret News*. The sentence thus originally said, "Because of their Masonic character the ceremonies of the temple are sacred and not for the public."[141] The word *Masonic* seems to have been intended by the First Presidency as a descriptive term for non-Mormons, not as an indicator of actual temple content. The entry for the word *Masonic* in *Webster's*

Third New International Dictionary of the English Language says that it means "suggestive of or resembling Freemasons or Freemasonry (as in display of fraternal spirit or secrecy)."[142]

Shortly after this history article was published in California, Charles W. Penrose was installed as the Second Counselor in the First Presidency. He authored an article for a Church magazine regarding a list of "peculiar questions" that had been submitted to the First Presidency. Question number sixteen was, "Why do the elders of your Church use Masonic signs and emblems, and has 'Mormonism' anything to do with Freemasonry?" President Penrose responded by saying, "We might answer: 'Because they don't.' Seriously, Elders or other ministers of the Church, as such, do not use any signs of secret orders. Some of our brethren may be or have been members of the Masonic society, but the Church has no connection with what is called 'Freemasonry.'"[143]

15. *Joseph Smith had knowledge of Freemasonry's secrets long before he was introduced to them in March 1842.*

Theorists have proposed that the Prophet must have clandestinely gained knowledge of Masonry's secrets before his induction either through observing public performances of the ritual which were meant to ridicule the Masons (such as those which were staged during the time of the William Morgan scandal) or by reading printed exposés on the subject or by talking to LDS Church members who were already part of the fraternity.

The weakness of these conjectures lies in the fact that evidence for them is singularly lacking. In fact, there is some evidence to the contrary. Elder Franklin D. Richards (nephew of inaugural endowment participant Willard Richards and an officiator in the Nauvoo Temple[144]) stated in a late nineteenth-century meeting of Church authorities that Joseph Smith "was aware that there were some things about Masonry which had come down from the beginning, and *he desired to know what they were*, hence the lodge" was established in Nauvoo.[145] This statement lends support to the idea that Joseph Smith did not become aware of Masonic secrets before the 15th and 16th of March 1842.

Another thing that needs to be remembered when considering the theory of pre-induction knowledge is that if any Mormon Mason had prematurely revealed the secrets of the Craft to the Prophet, that person would have been subjected to the consequences spelled out in the bylaws they signed when they became a Freemason. The bylaws of the Nauvoo Lodge put it this way: "Should any member disclose to any person other than Ancient York Masons, in good standing, any of the proceedings or transactions of this lodge, improper to be made public, he shall be suspended, expelled, or otherwise dealt with, at the discretion of the lodge."[146] Yet there is no evidence of any such action being taken against a Mormon Mason for making improper disclosures to Joseph Smith. Newel K. Whitney, Heber C. Kimball,[147] and Hyrum Smith were all present for both days of the Prophet's initiation. These men not only continued to attend the Nauvoo Lodge after that point in time, but they also continued to serve as officers of it as well. Hyrum was eventually promoted to be the Master of the lodge.[148] George Miller also attended the Nauvoo Lodge several times after the Prophet became a Mason,[149] and James Adams continued serving in his role as Deputy Grand Master of Illinois. At his death he was "buried with Masonic honors."[150] None of these men ever had any disciplinary action taken against them for improperly revealing Masonry's secrets to the Prophet Joseph Smith.

NOTES

1. *Times and Seasons,* vol. 3, no. 12, 15 April 1842, 763; hereafter cited as *T&S.*

2. See ibid., vol. 1, no. 12, October 1840, 178–79.

3. Ibid., vol. 2, no. 16, 15 June 1841, 451.

4. H. Michael Marquardt, comp., *Early Patriarchal Blessings of The Church of Jesus Christ of Latter-day Saints* (Salt Lake City: The Smith-Pettit Foundation, 2007), 214.

5. See *Millennial Star,* vol. 26, no. 36, 3 September 1864, 569; hereafter cited as *MS.*

6. Marquardt, comp., *Early Patriarchal Blessings of The Church of Jesus Christ of Latter-day Saints,* 216.

7. Dean C. Jessee, ed., *Personal Writings of Joseph Smith,* rev. ed. (Salt Lake City and Provo, UT: Deseret Book and Brigham Young University Press, 2002), 458, 460; hereafter cited as *PWJS.*

8. Andrew F. Ehat and Lyndon W. Cook, eds., *The Words of Joseph Smith: The Contemporary Accounts of the Nauvoo Discourses of the Prophet Joseph,* rev. ed. (Orem, UT: Grandin Books, 1990), 40–41; hereafter cited as *WJS.*

9. Scott G. Kenney, ed., *Wilford Woodruff's Journal* (Midvale, UT: Signature Books, 1985), 2:217.

10. Letter, Heber C. Kimball to Parley P. Pratt, 17 June 1842, Parley P. Pratt Papers, LDS Church Archives, Salt Lake City, Utah, cited in *Brigham Young University Studies,* vol. 15, no. 4, Summer 1975, 458; hereafter cited as *BYUS.*

11. That the type of Masonic ritual practiced in Nauvoo was Ancient York Masonry see *T&S,* vol. 3, no. 17, 1 July 1842, 843; Brigham H. Roberts, ed., *History of the Church* (Salt Lake City: Deseret News Press, 1930), 5:446; hereafter cited as *HC.*

12. See *BYUS,* vol. 12, no. 4, Summer 1972, 416, 419.

13. Francis de Paula Castells, *Origin of the Masonic Degrees* (Hackensack, NJ: Wehman Brothers, 1965), 20.

14. Articles of Union, article #2, in Harry L. Haywood and James E. Craig, *A History of Freemasonry* (New York: The John Day Company, 1927), 261.

15. Castells, *Origin of the Masonic Degrees,* 22.

16. *Sangamo Journal,* vol. 10, no. 46, 8 July 1842.

17. One of the definitions of *inspiration* in Noah Webster's 1828 English dictionary is "the infusion of ideas into the mind by the Holy Spirit" (Noah Webster, *An American Dictionary of the English Language* [New York: S. Converse, 1828], s.v., "inspiration," definition #3).

18. *Sangamo Journal,* vol. 10, no. 47, 15 July 1842.

19. John C. Bennett, *The History of the Saints* (Boston: Leland and Whiting, 1842), 276.

20. George D. Smith, ed., *An Intimate Chronicle: The Journals of William Clayton* (Salt Lake City: Signature Books and Smith Research Associates, 1995), 134.

21. See *T&S,* vol. 3, no. 10, 15 March 1842, foldout insert between pages 720 and 721; cf. Hugh W. Nibley, *The Message of the Joseph Smith Papyri: An Egyptian Endowment* (Salt Lake City and Provo, UT: Deseret Book and The Foundation For Ancient Research and Mormon Studies, 2005). "Studies of Egyptian temple ritual since the time of Joseph Smith have revealed parallels with Latter-day Saint temple celebrations and doctrine, including a portrayal of the creation and fall of mankind, washings and anointings, and the ultimate return of individuals to God's presence. Moreover, husband, wife, and children are sealed together for eternity, genealogy is taken seriously; people will be judged according to their deeds in this life, and the reward for a just life is to live in the presence of God forever with one's family. It seems unreasonable to suggest that all such parallels occurred by mere chance" (Daniel H. Ludlow, ed., *Encyclopedia of Mormonism* [New York: Macmillan, 1992], 1:137); hereafter cited as *EM.*

22. See JST, Ex. 34:1–2.

23. *T&S*, vol. 2, no. 16, 15 June 1841, 451.

24. See John W. Gunnison, *The Mormons, or Latter-day Saints, in the Valley of the Great Salt Lake* (Philadelphia: Lippincott and Grambo, 1852), 59–60; *Woman's Exponent*, vol. 7, no. 14, 15 December 1878, 105; H. Donl Peterson, *Moroni: Ancient Prophet, Modern Messenger* (Bountiful, Utah: Horizon, 1983), 165.

25. *MS*, vol. 15, no. 30, 23 July 1853, 482.

26. A sermon delivered by Joseph Smith at the Nauvoo Temple site on 11 June 1843 clearly illustrates his view on the origin of the Nauvoo Temple ordinances—God and not man. An amalgamated text of parts of this sermon will serve to establish this point. Joseph taught: "The order and ordinances of the kingdom [of God] were instituted by the Priesthood in the council of heaven before the world was." "God has not changed the ordinances and priesthood." These ordinances pertain to "the salvation of man." "[T]here are certain ordinances and principles that, when they are taught and practiced, must be done in a place or house built for that purpose." Jesus Christ tried to gather the Jews of His day in order to perform the ordinances of "baptism for the dead, washing[s], anointings, etc." including the bestowal of certain "Priesthood revelations." However, the Jews "refused to be gathered that the fulness of the Priesthood might be revealed among them." Nevertheless, on the day of Pentecost "God obtained a house where Peter was[hed] and ano[inte]d, etc." God has gathered the Saints together in the last days to build Him a temple and "prepare them for the ordinances and endowment, washings and anointings, etc." "Why gather the people together in [Nauvoo]? For the same purpose that Jesus wanted to gather the Jews, to receive the ordinances, the blessings, and the glories that God has in store for His Saints . . . [B]uild [the Nauvoo Temple] and receive the ordinances and blessings which God has in store for you." These "ordinances . . . are necessary preparations for the world to come" (*WJS*, 209–16).

27. See Daniel C. Peterson, "Notes on 'Gadianton Masonry'," in Stephen D. Ricks and William J. Hamblin, eds., *Warfare in the Book of Mormon* (Salt Lake City: Deseret Book and The Foundation for Ancient Research and Mormon Studies, 1990), 174–224; Daniel C. Peterson, "'Secret Combinations' Revisited," *Journal of Book of Mormon Studies,* vol. 1, no. 1, Fall 1992, 184–88; Paul Mouritsen, "Secret Combinations and Flaxen Cords: Anti-Masonic Rhetoric and the Book of Mormon," *Journal of Book of Mormon Studies,* vol. 12, no. 1, 2003, 64–77; Nathan Oman, "'Secret Combinations': A Legal Analysis," *FARMS Review,* vol. 16, no. 1, 2004, 49–73; Matthew B. Brown, "Girded about with a Lambskin," *Journal of Book of Mormon Studies,* vol. 6, no. 2, 1997, 124–51.

28. Richard Bushman, *Joseph Smith and the Beginnings of Mormonism* (Urbana: University of Illinois, 1984), 130–31.

29. See Richard L. Anderson, *Investigating the Book of Mormon Witnesses* (Salt Lake City: Deseret Book, 1981); Lyndon W. Cook, ed., *David Whitmer Interviews: A Restoration Witness* (Orem, UT: Grandin Book, 1991).

30. John R. Kohlenberger III and James A. Swanson, eds., *The Strongest Strong's Exhaustive Concordance of the Bible* (Grand Rapids, MI: Zondervan, 2001), 1412, word #4229.

31. See Emil Kautzsch, ed., *Gesenius' Hebrew Grammar,* rev. ed. (Oxford: Clarendon, 1970), 238.

32. *PWJS,* 148.

33. Devery S. Anderson and Gary James Bergera, eds., *Joseph Smith's Quorum of the Anointed 1842–1845: A Documentary History* (Salt Lake City: Signature Books, 2005), 3–4; text modernized and clarified.

34. See *BYUS,* vol. 21, no. 3, Summer 1981, 319–20. The belief that Joseph Smith latched on to Masonic vocabulary and ideology seems to be weakened by his own words spoken on 11 June 1843 (about one year and three months after he became a Mason). He said at that time, "I [am] a rough stone. The sound of the hammer and chisel was never heard on me, *nor never will*

be. I desire the learning and wisdom of heaven alone" (*WJS,* 209–10; emphasis added). If this happens to be a reference to the rough ashlar and perfect ashlar stones of Masonic philosophy and ritual then this statement could be interpreted as the Prophet's rejection of a man-made system of human progression in favor of one that was God-given.

35. See *EM,* 608.

36. See *WJS,* 132, 258–59, 319, 373; Arnold K. Garr, "Joseph Smith: Mayor of Nauvoo," *Mormon Historical Studies,* vol. 3, no. 1, Spring 2002, 33.

37. See *BYUS,* vol. 19, no. 3, Spring 1979, 363.

38. See ibid., vol. 34, no. 1, 1994, 95.

39. See *WJS,* 261, 320.

40. See *HC,* 4:491.

41. See *BYUS,* vol. 31, no. 1, Winter 1991, 71 n. 195.

42. See *HC,* 5:1.

43. See *WJS,* 122, 129.

44. See *Relief Society Magazine,* vol. 6, no. 3, March 1919, 129. The day when a group of women formed the initial idea for the Relief Society was 4 March 1842, thus predating the establishment of Freemasonry in Nauvoo (see Jill M. Derr, Janath R. Cannon, and Maureen U. Beecher, *Women of Covenant: The Story of Relief Society* [Salt Lake City: Deseret Book, 1992], 26).

45. Church Educational System, *Church History in the Fulness of Times: Student Manual,* 2d ed. (Salt Lake City: The Church of Jesus Christ of Latter-day Saints, 2003), 249.

46. See *Evening and Morning Star,* vol. 1, no. 6, November 1832, 46; vol. 1, no. 10, March 1833, 74; vol. 2, no. 18, March 1834, 138.

47. See *T&S,* vol. 1, no. 6, April 1840, 85.

48. See ibid., vol. 2, no. 24, 15 October 1841, 568.

49. See *Woman's Exponent,* vol. 12, no. 7, 1 September 1883, 51; hereafter cited as *WE*; *Relief Society Magazine,* vol. 6, no. 3, March 1919, 129.

50. See *Messenger and Advocate*, vol. 3, no. 4, January 1837, 441–42; hereafter cited as *M&A*; *T&S*, vol. 2, no. 10, 15 March 1841, 355.

51. *WJS*, 110.

52. *M&A*, vol. 2, no. 12, September 1836, 382.

53. Ibid., vol. 3, no. 1, October 1836, 399.

54. See ibid., vol. 3, no. 4, January 1837, 442; *T&S*, vol. 2, no. 10, 15 March 1841, 356.

55. See *WJS*, 105.

56. Ibid., 104–105.

57. See *EM*, 3:1200.

58. See *M&A*, vol. 3, no. 4, January 1837, 442.

59. See *T&S*, vol. 2, no. 10, 15 March 1841, 356.

60. Nauvoo Relief Society Minute Book, 86–88. 1842.

61. *HC*, 4:604.

62. See ibid., 4:608.

63. Ibid., 6:59. In 1857 Heber C. Kimball told a group of Saints that one of the reasons for them receiving their endowments was "to learn . . . to hold [their] tongues" (George D. Watt, ed., *Journal of Discourses* [Liverpool: Franklin D. and Samuel W. Richards, 1854–1886], 5:133; hereafter cited as *JD*).

64. *WE*, vol. 12, no. 7, 1 September 1883, 51.

65. See ibid., vol. 20, no. 19, 15 April 1892, 149.

66. Ibid., vol. 34, nos. 2–3, July/August 1905, 14.

67. See *JD*, 1:133; *Church News*, 17 July 1993, 5.

68. *Improvement Era*, October 1942, 630.

69. *Painesville Telegraph*, vol. 2, no. 20, 20 May 1836.

70. *The New York Evangelist*, vol. 6, no. 15, 9 April 1836.

71. *Ohio Watchman and Liberal Enquirer*, 20 August 1836.

72. See *HC*, 1:359–62.

73. See Asher Benjamin, *The American Builder's Companion*, 1806, reprinted (New York: de Capo Press, 1972); *The Practical House Carpenter*, 1830, reprinted (New York: De Capo Press, 1972); *Practice of Architecture*, 1833, reprinted (New York: De Capo Press, 1972).

74. *JD,* 13:357; emphasis added.

75. *HC,* 2:410; "the consecrated pulpits of the temple of the Lord" (*M&A,* vol. 3, no. 2, November 1836, 414).

76. See Smith, ed., *An Intimate Chronicle: The Journals of William Clayton,* 206.

77. Ibid.

78. For a survey of the artwork that decorated the celestial room of the Nauvoo Temple see *BYUS,* vol. 41, no. 2, 2002, 47–69.

79. See Yasha Beresiner, "Masonic Globes," Pietre-Stones Review of Freemasonry (website), Masonic Papers.

80. See *T&S,* vol. 2, no. 20, 16 August 1841, 517.

81. See Webster, *An American Dictionary of the English Language,* s.v., "mensuration."

82. See Commissioners of National Education, *A Treatise on Mensuration for the Use of Schools,* 2d ed. (Dublin, Ireland: John S. Folds, 1837), 125.

83. Smith, ed., *An Intimate Chronicle: The Journals of William Clayton,* 237.

84. See 2 Ne. 23:10; Hel. 14:20; 3 Ne. 8:22; D&C 29:14, 34:9, 45:42, 76:96–98, 88:45, 121:30, 128:23, 133:49; Moses 2:16.

85. See *PWJS,* 11.

86. See *HC,* 2:52.

87. See *Evening and Morning Star,* vol. 1, no. 9, February 1833, 72; Donald Q. Cannon and Lyndon W. Cook, eds., *Far West Record* (Salt Lake City: Deseret Book, 1983), 209.

88. Wandle Mace autobiography 207, Writings of Early Latter-day Saints, L. Tom Perry Special Collections, Harold B. Lee Library, Brigham Young University, Provo, Utah.

89. *M&A,* vol. 1, no. 7, April 1835, 100.

90. Marquardt, comp., *Early Patriarchal Blessings of The Church of Jesus Christ of Latter-day Saints,* 204, 205, 213.

91. *Pittsburgh Christian Advocate,* vol. 8, no. 28, 23 June 1841.

92. *The Overland Monthly*, vol. 16, no. 96, December 1890, 620.

93. *HC*, 6:196–97; cf. Ex. 25:9, 40; Num. 8:4.

94. Josiah Quincy, *Figures of the Past: From the Leaves of Old Journals* (Boston: Roberts Brothers, 1888), 389.

95. This inscription was planned for the Independence, Missouri temples (see *HC*, 1:359 and Appendix 3 of the present volume).

96. See Perrigrine Sessions, *The Diaries of Perrigrine Sessions*, vol. B (Bountiful, Utah: Carr, 1967), 43–44.

97. See Ex. 40:38; Lev. 16:4; Num. 10:8.

98. One of the original architectural drawings of the Nauvoo Temple that depicts the all-seeing eye in the fanlight section of the tall windows can be seen in Don F. Colvin, *Nauvoo Temple: A Story of Faith* (American Fork, UT: Covenant, 2002), 174. On 6 August 1845 Lyman O. Littlefield described the Nauvoo Temple symbols to Parley P. Pratt in a letter and referred to some "beautiful drops or Masonic emblems" (*New York Messenger*, vol. 2, no. 9, 30 August 1845, 68). Considering the context of the statement, he may be referring to the fact that the all-seeing eyes planned for the arches of the tall windows were actually installed. His belief that they were 'Masonic' may have been influenced by the fact that a large, prominently displayed, all-seeing eye decorated the east gable of Nauvoo's Masonic lodge.

99. See Glen M. Leonard, *Nauvoo: A Place of Peace, A People of Promise* (Salt Lake City and Provo, UT: Deseret Book and BYU Press, 2002), 253. The compass and square on the Nauvoo Temple weathervane drawing are not positioned in the typical Masonic configuration and, in fact, both of the planned Nauvoo Temple tools are pointing in different directions than the Masonic tools (as they are usually displayed).

100. See Laurel B. Andrews, *The Early Temples of the Mormons: The Architecture of the Millennial Kingdom in the American West* (New York: State University of New York Press, 1978), 90 and

Albert C. Stevens, ed., *The Cyclopaedia of Fraternities,* 2d ed. (New York: E. B. Treat and Company, 1907), 71.

101. See Appendix 3 of the present volume.

102. See *T&S,* vol. 6, no. 5, 15 March 1845, 844.

103. See the timeline in chapter 5 of the present volume.

104. Geneva Bible, 1599, 1 Corinthians 3:3, n. 1d, "By the square and compass of man's wit and judgment." A connection between architectural tools and human attributes is something that Freemasons would place emphasis on in later centuries.

105. Wandle Mace autobiography, 207, Writings of Early Latter-day Saints, L. Tom Perry Special Collections, Harold B. Lee Library, Brigham Young University, Provo, Utah.

106. *The Overland Monthly,* vol. 16, no. 96, December 1890, 620.

107. *New York Spectator,* 9 November 1844.

108. *T&S,* vol. 5, no. 19, 15 October 1844, 675.

109. The presence of the compass and square on the planned exteriors of the Nauvoo and Salt Lake temples may possibly be explained by the fact that Brigham Young delighted in referring to the LDS temple ordinances as "Celestial Masonry." The display of these emblems may have been his way of giving the outside world a message about the nature of what went on inside those buildings. This perspective may also help to explain why President Young wore a Masonic compass and square pin in a few of his Utah-era photographs. Or, he may have worn the pin in order to remind other Americans that he was part of a brotherhood that was bound by oath to look after its own (see Wilford Woodruff Journal, 19 August 1860).

110. See Appendix 3 of the present volume.

111. See the letter by Truman O. Angell, Sr. to President John Taylor, 29 April 1886, John Taylor Papers, LDS Church Archives, Salt Lake City, Utah.

112. Webster, *An American Dictionary of the English Language,* s.v., "degree," definition #1.

113. John D. Lee became a Freemason in August 1842 (PDF communication from the Grand Lodge of Illinois, 23 April 2009).

114. Smith, ed., *An Intimate Chronicle: The Journals of William Clayton*, 215.

115. Ibid., 216, 233, 237.

116. See *HC,* 2:367, 371, 389, 410, 433.

117. See ibid., 7:535, 554.

118. *JD,* 11:328.

119. Ibid., 18:303.

120. *BYUS*, vol. 15, no. 4, Summer 1975, 458.

121. Elder Kimball wrote: "Bro[ther] Joseph says Masonry was taken from Priesthood." Though there is no direct descent of Masonic rituals from the temple built by King Solomon the student of biblical ritual (Old and New Testaments), and early Christian rites should be able to discern that there is an indirect link between the fundamental elements of the Masonic ceremonies and what took place in the past.

122. S. Brent Morris, *The Complete Idiot's Guide to Freemasonry* (New York: Alpha Books, 2006), 129–30.

123. *BYUS,* vol. 15, no. 4, Summer 1975, 458.

124. Stan Larsen, ed., *A Ministry of Meetings: The Apostolic Diaries of Rudger Clawson* (Salt Lake City: Signature Books and Smith Research Associates, 1993), 42.

125. Ann Eliza Young, *Wife No. 19* (Hartford, CT: Dustin, Gilman and Company, 1875), 371. This book was written (as noted on the title page) by "Brigham Young's Apostate Wife."

126. Helen Marr Whitney, *Why We Practice Plural Marriage* (Salt Lake City: Juvenile Instructor Office, 1884), 63.

127. *Salt Lake Tribune,* 8 October 1870, 5.

128. Larsen, ed., *A Ministry of Meetings: The Apostolic Diaries of Rudger Clawson,* 380.

129. The statement under discussion is sometimes erroneously attributed to Eliza R. Snow.

130. See Edward W. Tullidge, *The Women of Mormondom* (New York: Tullidge and Crandall, 1877), 75, 79.

131. See Ronald W. Walker, "Edward Tullidge: Historian of the Mormon Commonwealth," *Journal of Mormon History*, vol. 3, 1976, 55–72.

132. Tullidge, *The Women of Mormondom*, 195.

133. Ibid., 176.

134. Ibid., 192.

135. Ibid., 23.

136. See James B. Allen and Glen M. Leonard, *The Story of the Latter-day Saints*, 2d ed. (Salt Lake City: Deseret Book, 1992), 688.

137. Edward W. Tullidge, *Life of Joseph the Prophet* (New York: Tullidge and Crandall, 1878), 391–92.

138. Edward W. Tullidge, *Tullidge's Histories* (Salt Lake City: Juvenile Instructor Office, 1889), 2:445.

139. Ibid., 2:426.

140. James R. Clark, ed., *Messages of the First Presidency of The Church of Jesus Christ of Latter-day Saints* (Salt Lake City: Bookcraft, 1970), 4:250.

141. *Oakland Tribune*, 15 October 1911, 36.

142. Philip B. Gove, ed., *Webster's Third New International Dictionary of the English Language* (G. & C. Merriam Company, 1961), s.v., "masonic."

143. *Improvement Era*, September 1912, 1045.

144. Smith, ed., *An Intimate Chronicle: The Journals of William Clayton*, 216.

145. Larsen, ed., *A Ministry of Meetings: The Apostolic Diaries of Rudger Clawson*, 42; emphasis added.

146. Mervin B. Hogan, *The Founding Minutes of Nauvoo Lodge* (Des Moines, IA: Research Lodge Number 2, 1971), 5.

147. Heber C. Kimball declared after the Prophet's death in 1844: "I have been as true as an angel from the heavens to the covenants I made in the lodge at Victor" in 1823 (*WE*, vol. 9, no. 20, 15 March 1881, 154).

148. See Hogan, *The Founding Minutes of Nauvoo Lodge,* 15–19, etc.

149. See ibid., 23, 26, 29.

150. *HC,* 5:85, 537.

APPENDIX 1

Early Mormon Symbolism

When some people look at the symbols on the exterior of the Salt Lake Temple they automatically think that they must have Masonic meanings since the Freemasons use them and since the Mormons were once closely connected with that fraternity. This appendix is designed to show that members of The Church of Jesus Christ of Latter-day Saints were aware of and incorporated these symbols into their culture long before the introduction of a Masonic lodge in Nauvoo, Illinois, in March 1842. In the chapter in the present volume on mythology it was demonstrated that some of the symbols on the exterior of the Nauvoo Temple were shown to Joseph Smith in a divine vision. It should also be noted here that Brigham Young and Wilford Woodruff both claimed to have had a vision of the Salt Lake Temple before it began to be constructed, though there is no indication that they were shown a detailed symbolic program in connection with that building.[1]

ALL-SEEING EYE

1828–29 – "I pray the God of my salvation that He view me with His all-searching eye" (2 Ne. 9:44).

1828–29 – "under the glance of the piercing eye of the Almighty God" (Jacob 2:10).

1828–29 – "the glance of [God's] all-searching eye" (Mosiah 27:31).

December 1830 – "I can stretch forth mine hands and hold all the creations which I have made; and mine eye can pierce them also" (Moses 7:36).

2 January 1831 – "Thus saith the Lord your God, even Jesus Christ, the Great I AM, Alpha and Omega, the beginning and the end, the same which looked upon the wide expanse of eternity, and all the seraphic hosts of heaven, before the world was made; The same which knoweth all things, for all things are present before mine eyes. . . . mine eyes are upon you. I am in your midst and ye cannot see me" (D&C 38:1–2, 7).

13 August 1831 – "mine eyes are upon those who have not as yet gone up unto the land of Zion" (D&C 62:2).

1 November 1831 – "Hearken, O ye people of my church, saith the voice of Him who dwells on high, and whose eyes are upon all men" (D&C 1:1).

November 1831 – "Behold and lo, mine eyes are upon you" (D&C 67:2).

31 July 1832 – "my heart is naked before [God's] eyes continually."[2]

4 January 1833 – "the eyes of my Maker are upon me."[3]

May 1835 – "the scrutinizing eye of 'Him with whom we have to do.'"[4]

29 January 1836 – "[the] Lord had [His] eye upon thee."[5]

9 May 1836 – "they stand naked and exposed to the piercing eye of Jehovah."[6]

May 1836 – "God is not mocked with impunity. His all seeing eye beholds you at all times. . . . His all-seeing eye surveys the whole of His vast creation."[7]

April 1837 – "the scrutinizing eye of Jehovah is ever upon them."[8]

June 1837 – "In vain do they attempt to hide from the scrutinizing eye of Jehovah."[9]

20 March 1839 – "Behold, mine eye seeth and knoweth all their works."[10]

3 July 1839 – "the God of Jacob has His eye upon you."[11]

September 1840 – "the all-searching eye of an Omnipresent God."[12]

January1841 – "God that sheweth mercy; having His eye at the same time directed towards His covenant people."[13]

13 December 1841 – "Let it not be supposed that the sick and the destitute are to be denied the blessings of the Lord's house; God forbid; His eye is ever upon them for good."[14]

HANDCLASP

26 April 1832 – "The right hand of fellowship [was] given to [Joseph Smith Jr.] by the bishop, Edward Partridge, in the land of Zion in the name of the Church" on 25 January 1832.[15]

31 July 1832 – Joseph Smith had a scribe write in a letter to the Saints in Independence, Missouri, "all those among you who are iniquitous persons and rebellious . . . do not have my right hand of fellowship."[16]

24 November 1835 – Joseph Smith Jr. performed a marriage ceremony "by the authority of the everlasting priesthood." He requested the bride and groom to "join hands," and then they entered into a "covenant" while the Prophet pronounced "the blessings that the Lord conferred upon Adam and Eve."[17]

16 January 1836 – The First Presidency and Quorum of the Twelve Apostles "took each other by the hand in confirmation of [their] covenant" with each other.[18]

23 November 1837 – "The Elders' quorum met in the Lord's house . . . . [A] difficulty between [some Elders] . . . was brought before the quorum and settled satisfactorily and [the Elders then] shook hands in token of fellowship."[19]

27 June 1839 – Joseph Smith taught the members of the First Presidency and Quorum of the Twelve Apostles one of "the keys of the kingdom of God" which was how to detect the nature of an otherworldly visitor by means of a handclasp.[20]

22 July 1840 – Joseph Smith Jr. had a scribe write in a letter to William W. Phelps, "I shall be happy once again to give you the right hand of fellowship."[21]

HOLINESS TO THE LORD

April 1830 – "walking in holiness before the Lord" (D&C 20:69).

6 April 1830 – "walking in all holiness before me" (D&C 21:4).

June–October 1830 – "walked in holiness before the Lord" (Moses 5:26).

2 January 1831 – "practice . . . holiness before me" (D&C 38:24).

February 1831 – "act in all holiness before me" (D&C 43:9).

8 March 1831 – "practice . . . holiness before me continually" (D&C 46:33).

3 November 1831 – "be sanctified in holiness before the Lord" (D&C 133:35).

27 March 1836 – "Thy house [is] a place of Thy holiness" (D&C 109:13).

January 1833 – The phrase, "HOLINESS TO THE LORD" is associated with the Second Coming and the establishment of Zion.[22]

25 June 1833 – The First Presidency of the Church wrote in a letter that each of the twenty-four temples in Jackson County, Missouri, was to be adorned with the inscription, "HOLINESS TO THE LORD."[23]

6 January 1836 – The phrase "holiness to the Lord" was invoked in connection with building "a city of righteousness."[24]

BEES

1829 – Honey bees called "deseret" (Ether 2:3).

November 1832 – The disciple of Jesus Christ is to have "industry" like the "bees."[25]

July 1833 – Mention of the "deseret" bees in the Book of Mormon.[26]

15 October 1841 – Mormons working on the Nauvoo Temple are said to be "busy as bees." Altogether the Saints appear to be an "industrious" group.[27]

NOTES

1. George D. Watt, ed., *Journal of Discourses* (Liverpool: Franklin D. and Samuel W. Richards, 1854–1886), 1:133; L. John Nuttal Papers, 7 October 1891. The symbols on the exterior of the Salt Lake Temple appear to be a modified and expanded version of the symbols associated with the Nauvoo Temple.

2. Letter by Joseph Smith Jr. in Dean C. Jessee, ed., *Personal Writings of Joseph Smith,* rev. ed. (Salt Lake City and Provo, UT: Deseret Book and BYU Press, 2002), 269; hereafter cited as *PWJS.*

3. Letter by Joseph Smith Jr. in ibid., 298.

4. Statement by Oliver Cowdery in *Messenger and Advocate,* vol. 1, no. 8, May 1835, 121; hereafter cited as *M&A.*

5. Joseph Smith Sr. statement in Dean C. Jessee, Mark Ashurst-McGee, and Richard L. Jensen, eds., *The Joseph Smith Papers: Journals Volume 1, 1832–1839* (Salt Lake City: The Church Historian's Press, 2008), 176.

6. Letter by Parley P. Pratt dated 9 May 1836 in *M&A,* vol. 2, no. 8, May 1836, 318.

7. Remark by John Whitmer in ibid., 306.

8. Statement by William Marks in ibid., vol. 3, no. 7, April 1837, 493.

9. Comment by William Marks in ibid., vol. 3, no. 9, June 1837, 525.

10. Letter by Joseph Smith Jr. in *PWJS,* 435.

11. Epistle of the Quorum of the Twelve Apostles signed by Brigham Young, Heber C. Kimball, John E. Page, Wilford Woodruff, John Taylor, and George A. Smith in Brigham H. Roberts, ed., *History of the Church* (Salt Lake City: Deseret News Press, 1930), 3:394; hereafter cited as *HC.*

12. Orson Pratt, *An Interesting Account of Several Remarkable Visions* (Edinburgh: Ballantyne and Hughes, 1840), 27.

13. Article by Brigham Young and Willard Richards in *Millennial Star,* vol. 1, no. 9, January 1841, 223.

14. Epistle of the Quorum of the Twelve Apostles signed by Brigham Young, Heber C. Kimball, Orson Pratt, William Smith, Lyman Wight, Wilford Woodruff, John Taylor, George A. Smith, and Willard Richards in *Times and Seasons,* vol. 3, no. 4, 15 December 1841, 626. Notice that the all-seeing eye is being indirectly connected with the temple.

15. Donald Q. Cannon and Lyndon W. Cook, eds., *Far West Record: Minutes of The Church of Jesus Christ of Latter-day Saints 1830–1844* (Salt Lake City: Deseret Book, 1983), 44.

16. *PWJS,* 271.

17. Jessee, Ashurst-McGee, and Jensen, eds., *The Joseph Smith Papers: Journals Volume 1, 1832–1839,* 109–110.

18. Ibid., 160.

19. Lyndon W. Cook and Milton V. Backman Jr., eds., *Kirtland Elders' Quorum Record 1836–1841* (Provo, UT: Grandin Book, 1985), 34.

20. Andrew F. Ehat and Lyndon W. Cook, eds., *The Words of Joseph Smith: The Contemporary Accounts of the Nauvoo Discourses of the Prophet Joseph* (Orem, UT: Grandin Book, 1991), 6, see also 12 (before 8 August 1839), 44 (December 1840), and 66 (21 March 1841); cf. D&C 129.

21. *PWJS,* 509.

22. *Evening and Morning Star,* vol. 1, no. 8, January 1833, 63; hereafter cited as *EMS.*

23. *HC,* 1:359.

24. *M&A,* vol. 2, no. 4, January 1836, 245.

25. *EMS,* vol. 1, no. 6, November 1832, 47.

26. Ibid., vol. 2, no. 14, July 1833, 107.

27. *Times and Seasons,* vol. 2, no. 24, 15 October 1841, 580.

APPENDIX 2

An LDS View of Derivation

Following are seven statements by Latter-day Saints that establish the viewpoint of some nineteenth century Mormons with regard to the origin of Freemasonry. The first statement comes from Joseph Smith's scribe Willard Richards and was written by him on or very near the day when the Prophet was raised to the degree of Master Mason. The statements by Heber C. Kimball (a contemporary record) and Benjamin F. Johnson (a reminiscent account) reflect the thought of Joseph Smith on the matter.

The message behind all of these statements is consistent—There are similarities between Freemasonry and the Mormon endowment because Masonry is a product of apostasy or degeneration from a priesthood-based prototype. Latter-day Saints possess the authentic version.

Willard Richards (16 March 1842): "Masonry had its origin in the Priesthood. A hint to the wise is sufficient."[1]

Heber C. Kimball (17 June 1842): "There is a similarity of priesthood in Masonry. Brother Joseph [Smith] says Masonry was taken from priesthood."[2]

Benjamin F. Johnson (1843): Joseph Smith "told me Freemasonry, as at present, was the apostate endowments, as sectarian religion was the apostate religion."[3]

Joseph Fielding (December 1843): The LDS temple ordinances are "the true origin of Masonry."[4]

Saints in Salt Lake City (1849–50): "Masonry was originally of the church, and one of its favored institutions, to advance the members in their spiritual functions. It had become perverted from its designs."[5]

Heber C. Kimball (9 November 1858): "The Masonry of today is received from the apostasy. . . . They have now and then a thing that is correct, but we have the real thing."[6]

Church Authorities (1842–1873): "The Mormon leaders have always asserted that Free-Masonry was a . . . degenerate representation of the order of the true priesthood."[7]

NOTES

1. Letter, 7–25 March 1842, Willard Richards to Levi Richards, published in Joseph Grant Stevenson, ed., *Richards Family History* (Provo, UT: Stevenson's Genealogical Center, 1991), 3:90.

2. Stanley B. Kimball, *Heber C. Kimball: Mormon Patriarch and Pioneer* (Urbana, IL: University of Illinois Press, 1981), 85.

3. Benjamin F. Johnson, *My Life's Review* (Heber City, UT: Archive Publishers, 2001), 113.

4. *Brigham Young University Studies,* vol. 19, no. 2, Winter 1979, 145; hereafter cited as *BYUS.*

5. John W. Gunnison, *The Mormons, or Latter-day Saints, in the Valley of the Great Salt Lake* (Philadelphia: Lippincott and Company, 1856), 59.

6. *BYUS,* vol. 15, no. 4, Summer 1975, 458.

7. Thomas B. H. Stenhouse, *The Rocky Mountain Saints* (New York: D. Appleton and Company, 1873), 698.

SELECTED BIBLIOGRAPHY

BOOKS

Allen, James B. and Glen M. Leonard, *The Story of the Latter-day Saints,* 2d ed. (Salt Lake City: Deseret Book, 1992).

Anderson, Devery S. and Gary James Bergera, eds., *Joseph Smith's Quorum of the Anointed 1842–1845: A Documentary History* (Salt Lake City: Signature Books, 2005).

Andreopoulos, Andreas, *Metamorphosis: The Transfiguration in Byzantine Theology and Iconography* (Crestwood, New York: St. Vladimir's Seminary Press, 2005).

Andrews, Carol, *Amulets of Ancient Egypt* (Austin: University of Texas Press, 1994).

Andrews, Laurel B., *The Early Temples of the Mormons: The Architecture of the Millennial Kingdom in the American West* (New York: State University of New York Press, 1978).

Anglicus, Galfridus and Albert Way, eds., *Promptorium Parvulorum Sive Clericorum: Lexicon Anglo-Latinum Princeps* (London: Camden Society, 1843).

Anonymous, *A Complete Account of the Ceremonies Observed in the Coronations of the Kings and Queens of England,* 4th ed. (London: Roberts, Stagg, and Browne, 1727).

Applebaum, Herbert, *The Concept of Work* (New York: State University of New York Press, 1992).

Bagnall, Roger S., ed., *Egypt in the Byzantine World 300–700* (New York: Cambridge University Press, 2007).

Bak, János M., ed., *Coronations: Medieval and Early Modern Monarchic Ritual* (Berkeley: University of California Press, 1990).

Bar-Asher, Moshe, et al., eds., *Studies in the Bible, Its Exegesis and Language* (Jerusalem: Mosad Bialik, 2007).

Bateman, Newton, ed., *Historical Encyclopedia of Illinois* (Chicago: Munsell, 1912).

Benjamin, Asher, *The American Builder's Companion,* 1806, reprinted (New York: de Capo Press, 1972).

_____. *The Practical House Carpenter,* 1830, reprinted (New York: De Capo Press, 1972).

_____. *Practice of Architecture,* 1833, reprinted (New York: De Capo Press, 1972).

Benson, Ezra Taft, *The Teachings of Ezra Taft Benson* (Salt Lake City: Bookcraft, 1988).

Black, Susan E. and Larry C. Porter, eds., *Lion of the Lord: Essays on the Life and Service of Brigham Young* (Salt Lake City: Deseret Book, 1995).

Brecht, Martin, *Martin Luther: His Road to Reformation, 1483–1521* (Minneapolis: Fortress Press, 1985).

Brown, Matthew B., *The Gate of Heaven: Insights on the Doctrines and Symbols of the Temple* (American Fork, UT: Covenant, 1999).

Burmester, Oswald, trans., *Ordination Rites of the Coptic Church* (Cairo: Society of Coptic Archeology, 1985).

Bushman, Richard, *Joseph Smith and the Beginnings of Mormonism* (Urbana: University of Illinois, 1984).

Cannon, Donald Q., and Lyndon W. Cook, eds., *Far West Record: Minutes of The Church of Jesus Christ of Latter-day Saints, 1830–1844* (Salt Lake City: Deseret Book, 1983).

Carr, Harry, *The Freemason at Work*, 6th ed. (London: Lewis Masonic, 1981).

Carter, Kate B., comp., *Our Pioneer Heritage* (Salt Lake City: Daughters of Utah Pioneers, 1967).

Castells, Francis de Paula, *Origin of the Masonic Degrees* (Hackensack, NJ: Wehman Bros., 1965).

Charles, Robert H., *A Critical and Exegetical Commentary on the Revelation of St. John* (Edinburgh: T. & T. Clark, 1985).

Clark, James R., ed., *Messages of the First Presidency of The Church of Jesus Christ of Latter-day Saints* (Salt Lake City: Bookcraft, 1970).

Coil, Henry W., *Coil's Masonic Encyclopedia* (New York: Macoy Publishing and Masonic Supply Company, 1961).

Coldstream, Nicola, *Medieval Architecture* (New York: Oxford University Press, 2002).

Collins, John J., *The Scepter and the Star: The Messiahs of the Dead Sea Scrolls and Other Ancient Literature* (New York: Doubleday, 1995).

Colvin, Don F., *Nauvoo Temple: A Story of Faith* (American Fork, UT: Covenant, 2002).

Cook, Lyndon W., *Revelations of the Prophet Joseph Smith* (Salt Lake City: Deseret Book, 1985).

_____. and Milton V. Backman Jr., eds., *Kirtland Elders' Quorum Record, 1836–1841* (Provo, UT: Grandin Book, 1985).

Cooper, Robert L. D., *Cracking the Freemasons Code* (New York: Atria Books, 2006).

Cox, Trenchard, *Jehan Foucquet: Native of Tours* (Freeport, NY: Books for Libraries Press, 1972).

De Hoyos, Art and S. Brent Morris, eds., *Freemasonry in Context: History, Ritual, Controversy* (Lanham, MD: Lexington Books, 2004).

Dyer, Colin F. W., *Symbolism in Craft Freemasonry* (London: Lewis Masonic, 1983).

Edersheim, Alfred, *The Temple: Its Ministry and Services,* rev. ed. (Peabody, MA: Hendrickson, 1994).

Ehat, Andrew F. and Lyndon W. Cook, eds., *The Words of Joseph Smith: The Contemporary Accounts of the Nauvoo Discourses of the Prophet Joseph,* rev. ed. (Orem, UT: Grandin Books, 1991).

Faivre, Antoine and Wouter J. Hanegraff, eds., *Western Esotericism and the Science of Religion* (Leuven: Peeters, 1998).

Fawcett, Jane, *Historic Floors: Their Care and Conservation* (Oxford: Butterworth-Heinemann, 2001).

Ferguson, Everett, ed., *Encyclopedia of Early Christianity,* 2d ed. (New York: Garland Publishing, 1999).

Garrett, H. Dean, ed., *Regional Studies in Latter-day Saint History: Illinois* (Provo, UT: BYU Department of Church History and Doctrine, 1995).

Gould, Robert F., *The Four Old Lodges: Founders of Modern Freemasonry and Their Descendants* (London: Spencer's Masonic Depot, 1879).

_____. *The History of Freemasonry: Its Antiquities, Symbols, Constitutions, Customs, Etc.* (London: Thomas C. Jack, 1885).

_____. *The Concise History of Freemasonry* (Whitefish, MT: Kessinger Publishing, 1994).

Gove, Philip B., ed., *Webster's Third New International Dictionary of the English Language* (G. & C. Merriam Company, 1961).

Green, Ian M., *Print and Protestantism in Early Modern England* (New York: Oxford University Press, 2000).

Grosart, Alexander B., ed., *The Complete Works of Andrew Marvell* (New York: AMS Press, 1966).

Guillim, John, *A Display of Herladrie* (London: William Hall, 1611).

Gunkel, Hermann, *Creation and Chaos in the Primeval Era and the Eschaton* (Grand Rapids, MI: Eerdmans, 2006).

Gunnison, John W., *The Mormons, or Latter-day Saints, in the Valley of the Great Salt Lake* (Philadelphia: Lippincott and Grambo, 1852).

Hamblin, William J. and David R. Seely, *Solomon's Temple: Myth and History* (New York: Thames and Hudson, 2007).

Hamill, John, *Masonic Perspectives* (Australia: Victorian Lodge of Research, 1992).

_____ and Robert Gilbert, eds., *Freemasonry: A Celebration of the Craft* (London: Mackenzie Publishing, 1992).

Haywood, Harry L. and James E. Craig, *History of Freemasonry* (Whitefish, MT: Kessinger Publishing, 2003).

Herwaarden, Jan van, *Between James and Erasmus: Studies in Late Medieval Religious Life, Devotion and Pilgrimage in the Netherlands* (Leiden: Brill, 2003).

Hogan, Mervin B., *The Founding Minutes of Nauvoo Lodge* (Des Moines, IA: Research Lodge Number 2, 1971).

Hooper, Franklin, ed., *The Encyclopaedia Britannica*, 14th ed. (New York: Encyclopaedia Britannica, Inc., 1932).

Horne, Alex, *Sources of Masonic Symbolism* (Richmond, VA: Macoy Publishing, 1981).

Jacob, Margaret C., *Living the Enlightenment: Freemasonry and Politics in Eighteenth-Century Europe* (New York: Oxford University Press, 1991).

Jessee, Dean C., ed., *Papers of Joseph Smith* (Salt Lake City: Deseret Book, 1992).

_____. ed., *Personal Writings of Joseph Smith,* rev. ed. (Salt Lake City: Deseret Book, 2004).

_____. Mark Ashurst-McGee, and Richard L. Jensen, eds., *The Joseph Smith Papers: Journals Volume 1, 1832–1839* (Salt Lake City: The Church Historian's Press, 2008).

Johnson, Benjamin F., *My Life's Review* (Heber City, UT: Archive Publishers, 2001).

Kautzsch, Emil, ed., *Gesenius' Hebrew Grammar,* rev. ed. (Oxford: Clarendon, 1970).

Kenney, Scott G., ed., *Wilford Woodruff's Journal* (Midvale, UT: Signature Books, 1985).

Kimball, Stanley B., *Heber C. Kimball: Mormon Patriarch and Pioneer* (Urbana, IL: University of Illinois Press, 1981).

Knoop, Douglas D. and Gwilym P. Jones, *The Mediaeval Mason: An Economic History of English Stone Building in the Later Middle Ages and Early Modern Times* (Manchester: University of Manchester Press, 1933).

_____. *The Genesis of Freemasonry* (London: Q. C. Correspondence Circle, 1978).

Kohlenberger III, John R. and James A. Swanson, eds., *The Strongest Strong's Exhaustive Concordance of the Bible* (Grand Rapids, MI: Zondervan, 2001).

Krodel, Gottfried G. and Helmut T. Lehmann, eds., *Luther's Works* (Philadelphia: Fortress Press, 1972).

Larsen, Stan, ed., *A Ministry of Meetings: The Apostolic Diaries of Rudger Clawson* (Salt Lake City: Signature Books and Smith Research Associates, 1993).

Lee, Samuel, *Orbis Miraculum or The Temple of Solomon Portrayed by Scripture Light* (London: John Streater, 1659).

Legg, Leopold G. W., ed., *English Coronation Records* (Westminster: Archibald Canstable and Company, 1901).

Leonard, Glen M., *Nauvoo: A Place of Peace, A People of Promise* (Salt Lake City and Provo, UT: Deseret Book and BYU Press, 2002).

Lowden, John, *The Making of the Bibles Moralisées* (University Park, PA: Pennsylvania State University Press, 2000).

Ludlow, Daniel H., ed., *Encyclopedia of Mormonism* (New York: Macmillan, 1992).

Ludlow, Victor L., *Principles and Practices of the Restored Gospel* (Salt Lake City: Deseret Book, 1992).

Mackey, Albert G., *The Symbolism of Freemasonry* (New York: Clark and Maynard, 1869).

_____. *An Encyclopaedia of Freemasonry,* rev. ed. (New York: The Masonic History Company, 1921).

_____. *The History of Freemasonry: Its Legendary Origins* (New York: Gramercy Books, 1996).

MacNulty, W. Kirk, *Freemasonry: Symbols, Secrets, Significance* (New York: Thames and Hudson, 2006).

Markens, Isaac, *Abraham Lincoln and the Jews* (New York: Isaac Markens, 1909).

Marquardt, H. Michael, comp., *Early Patriarchal Blessings of The Church of Jesus Christ of Latter-day Saints* (Salt Lake City: The Smith-Pettit Foundation, 2007).

Martin, George M., comp., *British Masonic Miscellany* (Whitefish, MT: Kessinger Publishing, 2003).

Matthew, H. C. G. and Brian Harrison, eds., *Oxford Dictionary of National Biography* (New York: Oxford University Press, 2004).

McConkie, Bruce R., *Mormon Doctrine* (Salt Lake City: Bookcraft, 1966).

Morris, S. Brent, *The Complete Idiot's Guide to Freemasonry* (New York: Alpha Books, 2006).

Mounce, Robert H., *The Book of Revelation,* rev. ed. (Grand Rapids, MI: Eerdmans, 1997).

Muldowney, Mary S., trans., *Saint Augustine: Sermons on the Liturgical Seasons* (New York: Fathers of the Church, Inc., 1959).

Neale, John M. and Benjamin Webb, trans., *The Symbolism of Churches and Church Ornaments: A Translation of the First Book of the Rationale Divinorum Officiorum Written by William Durandus* (Leeds: T. W. Green, 1843).

Newton, Joseph F., *Modern Masonry: A Brief Sketch of the Craft Since 1717* (Washington, D.C.: The Masonic Service Association of the United States, 1924).

Nibley, Hugh W., *The Message of the Joseph Smith Papyri: An Egyptian Endowment* (Salt Lake City and Provo, UT: Deseret Book and The Foundation for Ancient Research and Mormon Studies, 2005).

Parry, Donald W., ed., *Temples of the Ancient World: Ritual and Symbolism* (Salt Lake City: Deseret Book, 1994).

Peterson, H. Donl, *Moroni: Ancient Prophet, Modern Messenger* (Bountiful, Utah: Horizon, 1983).

Pick, Fred L. and G. Norman Knight, *The Pocket History of Freemasonry*, 5th ed. (London: Frederick Muller, 1969).

Pratt, Orson, *An Interesting Account of Several Remarkable Visions* (Edinburgh: Ballantyne and Hughes, 1840).

Pratt, Parley P., *Key to the Science of Theology* (Liverpool: F. D. Richards, 1855).

_____. *Autobiography of Parley P. Pratt,* rev. ed. (Salt Lake City: Deseret Book, 2000).

Quincy, Josiah, *Figures of the Past: From the Leaves of Old Journals* (Boston: Roberts Brothers, 1883).

Ricks, Stephen D. and William J. Hamblin, eds., *Warfare in the Book of Mormon* (Salt Lake City and Provo, UT: Deseret Book and The Foundation for Ancient Research and Mormon Studies, 1990).

Rishel, Joseph J. and Suzanne L. Stratton, *The Arts in Latin America, 1492–1820* (Philadelphia, PA: Philadelphia Museum of Art, 2006).

Roberts, Alexander and James Donaldson, eds., *The Ante-Nicene Fathers* (Grand Rapids, MI: Eerdmans, 1956).

Roberts, Brigham H., ed., *History of the Church* (Salt Lake City: Deseret News Press, 1930).

Schaff, Philip and Henry Wace, eds., *Nicene and Post-Nicene Fathers,* 2d series (Oxford: Parker and Company, 1894).

Shann, G. V., trans., *Book of Needs of the Holy Orthodox Church* (New York: AMS Press, 1969).

Shepard, Alexandra, *Meanings of Manhood in Early Modern England* (New York: Oxford University Press, 2003).

Simons, Thomas G., *Holy People, Holy Place: Rites for the Church's House* (Chicago: Liturgy Training Publications, 1998).

Smith, Emma, comp., *A Collection of Sacred Hymns for the Church of the Latter Day Saints* (Kirtland, OH: Frederick G. Williams and Company, 1835).

Smith, William and Samuel Cheetham, eds., *A Dictionary of Christian Antiquities* (London: John Murray, 1875).

Stenhouse, Thomas B. H., *The Rocky Mountain Saints* (New York: D. Appleton and Company, 1873).

Stevens, Albert C., ed., *The Cyclopaedia of Fraternities,* 2d ed. (New York: E. B. Treat and Company, 1907).

Stevenson, David, *The Origins of Freemasonry: Scotland's Century, 1590–1710,* rev. ed. (Cambridge, MA: Cambridge University Press, 1990).

Stevenson, Joseph G., ed., *Richards Family History* (Provo, UT: Stevenson's Genealogical Center, 1991).

Stewart, Trevor, ed., *Freemasonry in Music and Literature* (London: Canonbury Masonic Research Centre, 2005).

Stillson, Henry L., ed., *History of the Ancient and Honorable Fraternity of Free and Accepted Masons* (Boston: The Fraternity Publishing Company, 1892).

Sturgis, Russell, *A Dictionary of Architecture and Building* (New York: Macmillan, 1901).

Tabbert, Mark A., *American Freemasons* (New York: New York University Press, 2005).

Taunton, Ethelred L., *The English Black Monks of St. Benedict* (New York: Longmans, Green and Company, 1897).

Thatcher, Oliver J. and Edgar H. McNeal, *A Source Book for Mediaeval History* (New York: Charles Scribner's Sons, 1905).

Tullidge, Edward W., *The Women of Mormondom* (New York: Tullidge and Crandall, 1877).

_____. *Life of Joseph the Prophet* (New York: Tullidge and Crandall, 1878).

_____. *Tullidge's Histories* (Salt Lake City: Juvenile Instructor Office, 1889).

Verheyen, Boniface, *The Holy Rule of St. Benedict* (Grand Rapids, MI: Christian Classics Ethereal Library, 1949).

Watt, George D., ed., *Journal of Discourses* (Liverpool, England: Franklin D. and Samuel W. Richards, 1854–1886).

Webster, Noah, *An American Dictionary of the English Language* (New York: S. Converse, 1828).

Whiston, William, ed., *The Works of Flavius Josephus* (Philadelphia: David McKay, 1890).

Whitaker, Edward C. and Maxwell E. Johnson, eds., *Documents of the Baptismal Liturgy*, rev. and exp. (Collegeville, MN: Liturgical Press, 2003).

Whitney, Helen M., *Why We Practice Plural Marriage* (Salt Lake City: Juvenile Instructor Office, 1884).

Whitney, Orson, F., *Life of Heber C. Kimball* (Salt Lake City: Juvenile Instructor Office, 1888).

Wilmhurst, Walter L., *The Meaning of Masonry: The Deeper Symbolism of Freemasonry* (Whitefish, MT: Kessinger Publishing, 1995).

Woolley, Reginald M., *Coronation Rites* (Cambridge, MA: University Press, 1915).

PERIODICALS

Ars Quatuor Coronatorum

Brigham Young University Studies

Church News

Conference Report

Deseret News

Deseret News Semi Weekly

Ensign

Evening and Morning Star

Heredom

Improvement Era

Journal of Book of Mormon Studies

Journal of Discourses

Juvenile Instructor

Messenger and Advocate

Metropolitan Museum of Art Bulletin

Millennial Star

New Era

New York Evangelist

New York Messenger

New York Spectator

Oakland Tribune

Ohio Watchman and Liberal Enquirer

Overland Monthly

Painesville Telegraph

Pittsburgh Christian Advocate

Salt Lake Tribune

Sangamo Journal

The Builder

The Return

Times and Seasons

Woman's Exponent

INDEX

England

legends of, combined with esoteric material from Scotland, 34

eternal marriage

concept of, known among LDS in 1835, 92

Joseph Smith taught, in 1839, 95

Faust, James E.

mysteries of existence answered in temples, 11

First Presidency

clarification on 1911 statement by, 156–57

Freemasonry

defined as a secular organization, 12

prerequisites for joining, 13

principles of, 14

no central group governs all of, 14

overall goal of, 15

change in nature of, after AD 1717, 15

only points toward life after death, 15

ritual elements of, not paralleled by LDS endowment, 22 n. 37

precise origins of, unknown, 27

Gilbert, Robert

theory of, on Roman Catholicism and Masonic rituals, 33

Grand Architect of the Universe

a Masonic reference for God, 46